CW00540055

Reviews

"The leading part of an advancing military formation is known as a vanguard. One of its functions is to seek out the enemy and secure ground in advance of the main force. This is what John Seddon and his colleagues from Vanguard have done, once again. Vanguard is at war with traditional management, and they are right there at the frontline, fighting outdated beliefs about management and leadership.

"In Beyond Command and Control, the thinking behind traditional management and the resulting practices are both ruthlessly challenged: budgets, targets, individual incentives, economy of scale and many others illusions of control and efficiency. Even Agile is challenged. Not the original intention behind it, but the industry it has developed into. This is all done with a sharp tongue, and with deep insights from years of hands-on studies of the real situation on the ground in a range of dysfunctional organisations.

"One day the main force will be able to move in, thanks to brave vanguards who dared to challenge accepted truths."
Bjarte Bogsnes, Chairman, Beyond Budgeting Institute

"Aviva PLC sees the change method described in these pages as a strategic signature – a way of improving how our organisation works through changing how all our leaders think. The Vanguard Method is fundamentally changing, for the better, what we can do for our customers and the culture within our business. This book provides insights and case studies of the impact John's approach brings to organisations looking to break out of conventional thinking."
Darren Cornish, Aviva PLC Group Director, Systems Thinking

"An essential read for all leaders - it will no doubt rock your long held beliefs of what we do as leaders - and it will allow you to discover how you truly can add value to your organisation and the populations you serve.

"Having worked with Vanguard and the systems thinking methodology for a number of years, I am able to appreciate what going on this

journey means for individuals. A few months into my journey, I was faced with a sudden realisation that my beliefs as a leader has been completely shattered. Not an easy experience to say the least - my foundations as a leader, that had been the bedrock of my practice for so long, seemed completely redundant and irrelevant. I also was a bit dumbfounded to say the least how on earth I had been able to fool myself for so long.

"There is such a temptation, in most organisations, and the public sector is no exception, when faced with difficult situations or challenges, to increase "grip and control", to increase scrutiny and challenge meetings, to ensure "important decisions" are made at the most senior level possible. In reality what we need to do as leaders it to "study the work" - to "study the demand for our services" - and by doing so, we create a whole new meaning for the word "management".

"If you are curious as to how you can lead differently - look no further than this book. If you are trying to transform services within your organisation, but see no real change in performance - look no further than this book. If you are asking yourself, why your change programmes have not delivered the change you envisaged or planned - then look no further than this book.

"My overwhelming wish as a leader is that more and more of us make the change as leaders - I cannot ever go back to managing and leading as I used to - but wouldn't it be great if the new way was the norm!"
Awen Morwena Edwards, Corporate Director and Statutory Director of Social Services, Gwynedd Council

"Demand is rising in Health and Social Care. We measure it all the time. It is our biggest concern; how will we cope? How will we manage the pressure on staff to prevent them leaving when totally disillusioned and burnt-out by the pace of work and the impossibility of "doing a good job" when it matters most? John and the Vanguard Method give us hope, and more than hope – they give us a method.

"Some leaders have paused and decided to stop "doing the wrong thing righter". Leaders who have been fortunate enough to work with John and his team have studied their own systems. They have learnt about the demand for their services, what constitutes value work,

and how well the current system achieves its purpose, as defined by the citizen. These leaders have developed an understanding of what matters to the people who need or chose to use their services, and they have learnt how the current system achieves or fails to meet citizen's needs. This gives a very different platform for redesigning services.

"Eliminating demand caused by failure in our health and care systems could provide a huge opportunity for us to improve people's experiences of care, and for people to achieve the outcomes that they value. Staff could have oodles more satisfaction at work, and by getting it right first time, by eliminating non value adding work, we could release resources to do better things. What are we waiting for?"
Iolanthe Fowler, Clinical Director Integrated Community Care and Primary Care Interface Services, Sheffield Teaching Hospitals Foundation Trust

"I've known John and his work for many years. The results his approach delivers are well known and widely lauded. As he writes "change is a normative process". That's to say, folks have to go see for themselves how things really are, and experience the dysfunctions of the status quo before becoming open to the possibilities of pursuing new ways of doing things. This resonates with my work in the Marshall Model, with command-and-control being a universal characteristic of Analytic-minded organisations and systems thinking being reserved to the Synergistic- and Chaordic-minded.

"One stand-out section of the book is the chapters explaining the role of software and IT systems. John echoes a now-common view in the software community regarding Agile software development and the wider application of Agile principles: "we soon came to regard this phenomenon [Agile] as possibly the most dysfunctional management fad we have ever come cross". These chapters give an insight into the progressive business perspective on the use of software and IT in business, in John's words "putting IT last". In mine: #NoSoftware."
Bob Marshall, Organisational Psychotherapist, Digital Transformation specialist and flow-chain sensei

"This book is an excellent guide for leaders using the Vanguard Method, it gets into the 'how' and 'why' of the Vanguard Method in practice. Explanations of how the method works are clear and the comparisons with conventional management thinking are detailed and illustrative

of the challenges in bringing new thinking into an organisation.

"I especially like the careful analysis of Agile. It highlights the perils in mistaking a technique for a method and how techniques can take on a life of their own in the hands of consultants seeking to earn a living.

"My favourite quote from the book: 'If you are doing the wrong thing without knowing it, you won't be able to get to the right thing by studying why the wrong thing went wrong.' This book will point you to the right thing."
Stephen Thorpe, Director, City Operations, Wyndham City, Australia

"This book teaches you how to create change that delights customers and employees alike. Customers feel well served and employees are allowed to use their brains without the corrupting influence of measures and standards. Understanding and fixing the system from the customer's perspective replaces the well-intentioned but misplaced manipulation of employees to do more of the wrong thing. Beware, this book will transform your organizational culture."
Walter Weber, President and CEO of UTEX Scientific, Ontario Canada

"Command and control has failed. For decades it has been taken for granted that this is the only way to get things done. It has been especially beloved by would-be-heroic leaders, on-the-make politicians, and back-watching bureaucrats. With its apparatus of standardisation, target-setting, budget management, coercion, inspection, and more recently digitisation, it promised efficiency, growth, and prosperity. Instead, it has produced a national productivity crisis, rising costs, failure demand, and services we should be ashamed of.

"But as John Seddon and his colleagues at Vanguard have shown, it need not be like this. Starting with a thorough understanding of what creates value for customers and communities, which can only be achieved by direct study, we can design systems which meet needs and drive down costs. For those who are already trying to work in this way, this important book will make you more determined, more confident that this is the direction to take. For those not yet on this journey it will be a revelation."
Steve Wyler, social change consultant, former CEO of Locality

Beyond Command
and Control

John Seddon et al

Printed by Mayfield Press

Published 2019

Printed and bound by Mayfield Press

ISBN: 978-1-5272-3956-2

Acknowledgements

Without clients none of this work would have been possible. While many first thought going beyond command and control would be a leap of faith they discovered that as it is based on getting knowledge it is actually a change based on informed choice. As well as leading profound change they had the courage to stand apart from the crowd.

Simon Caulkin (http://simoncaulkin.com), award-winning management journalist, management thinker and friend gave clarity and style to our prose. Brendan O'Donovan, Vanguard's head of research, brought his usual diligent attention as the book developed.

Contents

Contents

Introduction

Recalling two key interviews, the veteran BBC journalist and broadcaster Peter Day wrote:

> *"When I asked Marvin Bower [the architect of management consultancy McKinsey] what his main regret was in 60 years of advising the top people in first American and then global business, he did not hesitate in his reply: 'The prevalence of command and control,' he said.*
>
> *When I put the same question to Peter Drucker, his answer was immediate: 'I heartily agree with my friend Marvin Bower,' he said. A one-line answer that addressed the abiding problem of most organisations then and now."* *

The irony. One hundred years ago James McKinsey – he of the eponymous consulting firm – solved a problem that had been plaguing Alfred Sloan, the chairman and CEO of General Motors. With the invention of budget management, McKinsey provided a grateful Sloan with a means of bringing order to the amorphous mass that was the sprawling US car firm at the time. Unfortunately, he had also unknowingly created the keystone of the command-and-control management model lamented by Bower and Drucker, which is now as far beyond its sell-by date as house-sized gas-guzzlers with fins. Re-thinking McKinsey's century-old invention is fundamental to escaping – going beyond – the prison of command-and-control management.

Budget management is often described as management by the numbers. Those numbers are either financial or derived from financial measures which, as we shall show, are of no value in understanding and improving the system of work. Although it may seem normal to focus on managing finance, leaders sit astride a

---

* 'Selling Salvation' http://www.bbc.co.uk/radio4/features/in-business/peter-days-comment/20091224

system that, albeit unwittingly, they destabilise and sub-optimise by interfering with the way the system functions or, in simpler language, the way the work works. In effect, the purpose of the organisation is subverted into serving the controls, or "making the budget", which, as we will illustrate, severely constrains economic performance.

The dysfunctional consequences of using financial measures to manage by are ubiquitous and systemic. This is not because people are wicked – as managers sometimes assume – but because the requirement to serve the hierarchy and comply with conventional controls goes head to head with the requirements to serve customers. In a contest between using one's ingenuity for survival or improving service to the customer, we leave you to guess which will be the winner.

The consequence is that we have service organisations that are massively sub-optimised, offer poor service, depress the morale of those who work in them and are dominated by control mechanisms that not only do not contribute to improving the work, but actually make it worse.

The influential Gary Hamel argues for a root-and-branch re-think of management that would dethrone bureaucracy and its ideology of "controlism" as the default operating system.* He estimates that bureaucracy imposes excess costs of $3tn on US business alone. While the management principles that have guided the development of this default system seem logical, their plausibility is deceptive. Thus, it may be perfectly logical to want to control costs, but when it is appreciated that the ways we manage cost frequently has the opposite effect – increasing cost and pushing the system out of control – the mind is opened to a better logic for control.

The truth is that command-and-control management is the primary inhibitor to improving productivity and, hence, economic

---

* Hamel, G., First let's fire all the managers, HBR, Dec 2011

performance. But there is a better way to manage. Command and control is much more than budget management. So in chapter 1 we begin by defining command and control in order to begin to identify the many other practices and norms that make up command-and-control thinking.

In his 1966 book, Bower wrote:

> *"I believe that leaders and leadership teams working together in a proper design will run the business more effectively than by hierarchical, command-and-control managing. But I can't prove that. And there are no models."* *

This book provides Bower's missing model – more properly described as a method – one that has been tried and tested in many organisations across 11 countries, demonstrating profound results.

Bower emphasised two things: working together and a proper design. That leaders frequently don't work together may be a surprise to some. The reason is the way we think about control, which is central to the design. To give an egregious example: in one utility company the top 200 leaders had personal targets attached to large bonuses which were known to the individuals but kept secret, locked away in the HR department, from the others. It would be hard to imagine a more effective way of ensuring that people do not work together. We will return to dysfunctional effects of incentives later. Bower's second concern, a proper design, is the more critical issue, and the subject of this book.

The point is that the problem of people not working together won't be solved by interventions such as team-working, participation, empowerment programmes and the like, for one simple reason: it is the system that governs behaviour. As you will see, when the system changes, behaviour changes in tandem; and to change the system we have to change the way we think about management.

---

* Bower, M., (1966). *The Will to Manage: Corporate Success Through Programmed Management*. New York: McGraw-Hill

Changing the way we think about and conduct the practice of management is no less than a strategic imperative. This is not to say we shouldn't take account of competitors, markets and contextual issues. But it is to say that looking inside our own organisation provides a major strategic opportunity to make great strides. *It is also to assert that thinking differently about the purposes and practices of management is a profound lever.* As the focus of leaders shifts away from efficiency and turns instead to effectiveness, costs fall, competitive position strengthens, prices drop, sustainability improves, enterprises grow and create more jobs. It is top leadership's responsibility to unshackle their organisation from the current controls – which, after all, go right to the top – and institutionalise better ones.

There are now many organisations that have successfully applied the Vanguard Method and swear by it as the go-to method for change. It is common in a book like this to identify and cite such case studies of success. But for a number of reasons we have chosen not to do so.

First, naming the companies is likely to encourage "industrial tourism" – visiting to see what can be learned from them. But this is dangerously superficial, tempting visitors simply to map what they see on to their current mental models – the very thing that needs to change – without perceiving the deeper changes to the underlying thinking. This is what happened when UK business leaders travelled to Japan in the 1970s to learn the lessons of the "Japanese miracle". They copied the things they saw, such as suggestion schemes and problem-solving groups, but failed to appreciate the profoundly different way of thinking that underpinned the results.

Secondly, even successful change can be quickly undone by unsympathetic incoming management.

> *In the 1990s an office-supplies retailer applied our method with remarkable results. It was subsequently taken over by an American organisation whose leaders imposed what they*

described as "cookie-cutter" performance measures – the very controls that had been removed by the intervention when they were found to sub-optimise performance. When the UK leadership team tried to explain their misgivings, all examples of profound improvement using better controls were dismissed as "what managers are supposed to do" and the conventional (bad) measures mandated. The UK leaders promptly resigned.

Last year leaders who had applied the method in a financial services organisation were astonished to witness massive sub-optimisation created through the imposition of a "digital" strategy using Agile (lots more on these later). Again, their voices weren't heard, so they left.

Why is it that people's voices aren't heard when they try to explain results achieved by unconventional means? It is, quite simply, a matter of mental models.

A director of a financial services organisation became interested in the Vanguard Method. We took him out to study his organisation. He blogged about what he was learning and for his pains was fired "for criticising management". Despite this unfortunate start, we got to help the organisation change its approach. Years later, when the organisation decided to mandate the method across its worldwide operations, it sought a leader to make it happen – and re-hired the manager it had previously fired.

Managers who leave after adopting new mental models do so out of frustration at their failure to persuade others through reasoned argument, a phenomenon we expand on later. But the change of model is a Rubicon: so profound is the shift that no one who has made it will ever turn back to conventional command-and-control management.

The third reason for not naming companies is the corollary of the first: everything you need to know is there in your own system if you have eyes to see it. Learning how to see it is the crucial first step that managers must make if they are to unlearn the things they believe about management and learn new things that are counterintuitive. That is the most important theme running through this book, starting with chapter 2: The nature of the change. The remaining chapters of Part 1 explore what it means to cross the Rubicon, drawing on practical illustrations contrasting dysfunctional and functionally superior controls, and what it takes for leaders to make the crossing.

There are many organisations where the method is well embedded, and the examples in this book are drawn from them. But rather than consider the number of organisations that have employed the method, it is better to think about the sustainability of new mental models in terms of a ratchet: the steadily growing number of leaders who have crossed the river and cannot go back.

The opportunity extends beyond individuals and organisations. It is axiomatic that the collective performance of organisations, whether in the private or public sector, is central to economic performance, since wealth creation depends on enterprise. If every enterprise achieved the results shown by the trailblazers, we would have outstanding economic improvement. And this is no pipe dream. Unlike most books on management, this one is based squarely on evidence. The trailblazers are many; they all attest to levels of improvement beyond comparison, and all would insist upfront that they could not now go back to command-and-control management norms.

The journey beyond command and control is based on systems thinking. The start of this journey is to see, firstly, how current organisational performance is a consequence of patterns of (command-and-control) behaviour – how interactions and relationships between parts affect the whole. That might sound complicated, but in practice you will see that it is plain and simple. It is to appreciate how our current command-and-control mental models predictably create sub-optimal performance. What then follows is a clear focus on the most relevant relationships for building an enduring and profoundly better alternative. A distinctive difference from other systems approaches is a rejection of choosing a "future" or "desired" state and instead making what transpires emergent. A second difference is the emphasis on leaders engaging in the process of change directly, being hands-on, ensuring that they develop a common perspective, avoiding the problems associated with competing mental models.

While Part 1 of this book illustrates this systems approach in service operations – the places where an organisation makes or loses its fortunes and the necessary place to start – Part 2 moves on to address the burgeoning control bureaucracy that sits above operations, for that too has to change. We begin with how leaders approach change, before moving on to how to get real value from IT, with particular attention to Agile and digital services, and then addressing implications for HR policy and practice. Finally, in the Epilogue, we discuss how a mass movement across the Rubicon could help to solve the UK's much-pondered productivity conundrum.

To make a start, consider the following example. Straightforward as it is, it is useful for opening up issues with broader implications, many of which run through the more complex service cases that we explore later.

Think about what it would be like for you, the customer, to deal with a perfect service centre. You would call to request a service, and that's exactly what you would get, without fuss or frills. Note that this is *not* the norm today. To get what you want, you will usually have to call back, provide more information or ring another number. This is because giving customers what they want runs counter to the control logic at the heart of these organisations, and no amount of soothing slogans about customer service will change that. Central to the current management logic is the idea that better service requires more resources – bluntly, it costs more. So managers strictly control the time service centre agents spend talking to customers. In their minds, "giving customers what they want" would be the equivalent of suspending control and letting costs soar as a result.

Yet this logic – like many conventional management assumptions – is faulty. We will provide evidence to illustrate these flaws. As we do so, you will (we hope) learn how to study organisations, as this process – studying organisations from a fresh point of view – is, unusually, the way in which the journey beyond command and control begins.

Studying organisations from a different point of view inculcates a new way of thinking. Going beyond command and control means changing our assumptions about how to design and manage work. The power of this intellectual challenge creates urgency among leaders to make the necessary changes; this is what propels leaders to cross the Rubicon, and it gives them the means to design and manage an organisation which has the serving of customer demands as its *raison d'être*. This is not a slogan; it reflects a clear focus on a better purpose, using novel methods and controls. The consequent sustainability and agility is systemic; again, no slogan, for as customer demand changes the organisation is naturally attuned to adapt with it.

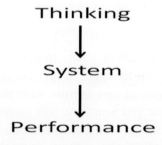

Understanding the relationship between management thinking, the system of organisation reflected in that thinking, and the organisational performance that results, is the Rubicon that you will cross. It is a two-step process that involves both un-learning and re-learning; discovering how command-and-control management introduces a range of conditions that sub-optimise performance is the preliminary to employing a better logic to design a different and more effective system of organisation. As you will see, the results that follow this change in thinking are nothing short of revolutionary.

Part 1:

Changing thinking about the management of service operations

1 What is command and control?

Ask people, "What is the problem with command and control?", and many will assume that the "command" word is the issue: it is about bosses being too bossy. If that is the case, the obvious antidote is for those higher up the hierarchy to be caring, to act as coach, to show more "respect" or to behave as "servants".

But there are times when leaders ought to be bossy.

The view that leaders should behave differently towards their people is widespread. The work of social psychologist Douglas McGregor was just one influence – as indicated by the title of his seminal work, *The Human Side of Enterprise*, one of the most influential management books of the last century. *

McGregor postulated two contrasting theories of people management, Theory X and Theory Y. Theory X says that employees need to be closely directed, monitored, and controlled to act in the interests of the firm, otherwise they will shirk. Theory Y is that employees want to do good work and can be trusted to do so. The popularity of this distinction led human resource departments to challenge management's assumptions about the motivations employees bring to their jobs. It also sparked what have been argued to be "innovations" in HR practice.

If the problem is seen to be managers making decisions while workers do as they are told, the antidote is to "empower" people.

---

* McGregor, D., (first published 1960). *The Human Side of Enterprise* (2006). New York: McGraw-Hill

The 1990s saw a large number of "empowerment" programmes, training courses designed to encourage empowered behaviour which usually, and ironically, ended with "how to have a negotiation with your boss". If the problem is thought to be lack of trust – managers can't trust their people to make decisions – the remedy is simply to trust people. So HR departments devised trust-building programmes. If the problem is perceived as a lack of respect or concern, the solution is for leaders to put their people first and/or to become "servant leaders".

This perspective fails to recognise the need to challenge the fundamental assumptions underpinning the prevailing management model. Empowerment is a "command-and-control" term – "I, the boss, empower you, the subordinate". Trust is not a point of intervention; it is the consequence of a good relationship. What colours the relationship between managers and workers is management's theories of control. To put it another way, what if, while intervening with coaching, empowerment, respect, trust or servant-leader programmes, the ways in which work is controlled doesn't change? What if faulty methods for control and decision-making are simply passed down the hierarchy in the name of these leadership / people-programmes?

For us, this is the point: Of the two words, command and control, it is "control" that is the more problematic.

Turning to another well-known motivational theorist, Fred Herzberg put it this way:

"If you want someone to do a good job, give them a good job to do" *

And that's the point; jobs in service organisations are not designed to be "good jobs"; the controls are not good controls.

---

* Herzberg. F., (1968). *'One more time: how do you motivate employees?'* Harvard Business Review, vol 46 no 1, Jan/Feb 1968

Our focus on organisation design and its determinant, management thinking, was inspired by the work of the US engineer, statistician and systems thinker, W. Edwards Deming, whose work we came across in the 1980s when we were asked to study the reasons for failure of many TQM (Total Quality Management) programmes. These programmes taught improvement techniques (tools) first developed in a few Japanese manufacturers. We learned that frequently the theories implicit in the tools were diametrically opposed to the theory of the organisation attempting to put them into practice – for example a focus on the process ran counter to the existing management by function.

What Deming pointed to was a wholly different management philosophy being employed, something largely missed by the large number of visitors who trooped off to Japan in search of the secret of the country's manufacturing's success. While many of the tourists set up quality circles and suggestion schemes on their return to the UK, they were put to work in systems that were incompatible with the underlying philosophy. Hence their failure. When asked what to do when an initiative failed, a US advocate of TQM, Phil Crosby, replied, "Do it again". We felt it was more important to find out the reasons for the failure.

Deming, who was lauded by Japanese manufacturers who'd followed his teaching, put it this way:

"Most people imagine that the present style of management has always existed, and is a fixture. Actually, it is a modern invention – a prison created by the way in which people interact." *

Deming is sometimes described as the "father of TQM". He would turn in his grave at such a thought. Fundamental to what he taught in Japan was that the organisation must be managed as a system. To that end, he argued that we must abandon the "present

---

* Deming, W.E., (1994). *The New Economics: For Industry, Government, and Education.* Massachusetts: MIT Press.

style of management", pointing to the obvious truth that since we, mankind, invented management, we could also reinvent it. Deming gave many examples of how to design and manage manufacturing organisations as systems, but few clues as to how to do that in service organisations – our focus. So that became the challenge. It is all the more important as although in all advanced economies the service sector has far outgrown manufacturing, its growth in size has not been matched by increasing effectiveness, to the detriment of our economies as a whole.

The "present style of management" is command and control, Deming's "prison" that prevents progress. By the 1990s, we had learned enough about all this to set out an operational definition of command and control. It is long, but necessarily so as it concerns the depth and breadth of the "present style of management":

Command and control: An operational definition

Command-and-control management is a top-down perspective in which:

- work is divided into functional specialisms
- decision-making is separated from work
- measures-in-use are related to the budget and arbitrary
- management's role is to "make the numbers" and "manage the people"
- workers' motivation is assumed to be extrinsic (carrot and stick)
- the attitude to suppliers and customers is contractual

The whole ethos is one of control, and the approach to change is to plan and project-manage any transformation.

To illustrate what command-and-control management looks like in more operational terms, let's return to our service centre. The focus of management is on transaction costs – for example, the time service-centre agents take in handling customers' calls. This was the founding rationale for creating service centres in the first place. Beginning in the 1980s, and facilitated by the advent of automated call distribution technology, managers moved "telephone work" out of departments or branches to specialist service centres. The Labour government under Tony Blair obliged UK local authorities to follow suit, a policy that was extended under successive governments to all UK public services.* While the official line was that standardisation and specialisation (as in Adam Smith's famous pin factory) would improve the quality of service to customers or citizens, the real motivation was to reduce costs.

The anticipated cost-reductions were the central feature of the plans and their associated budgets. In the service-centre case, the logic was (and still is) to count the number of calls handled in the original departments or branches, establish the time taken to deal with them and then use that as the basis for determining how many "seats" (agents) are required to handle the volume of work. The agents to be employed could be located in lower-wage-cost parts of the country and, later (when costs exceeded the budgeted plans – as they always did), lower-wage-cost countries.

The budgets were (and are) overspent because the volume of calls always exceeds the numbers in the plans. We saw this first in private-sector organisations in the 1980s, and the same thing duly occurred in the public sector in the decades following. Given management's logic – how many calls are coming in, how long does it take to handle them and thus how many people do I need? – the response to an increase in call volumes was (and is) to increase the headcount, bear down on agents to complete calls more quickly and further reduce the wage levels. The recent fashion for driving customers on to "digital channels" is predicated on the same assumption – that it will lower transaction costs – and, once again, the dysfunctional consequence is that the volume of work to do rises, something we return to later.

---

* Seddon, J., (2014). *The Whitehall Effect*, Triarchy Press.

Before explaining why the volume of transactions always increases, however, we will take a moment to explore the other aspects of command-and-control thinking that service-centre organisation displays. Specialisation and standardisation of work are of course assumed to reduce transaction costs, the former also cutting the need for training. Work specialisation also yields the opportunity to introduce interactive voice response (IVR – "press 1 for this, 2 for that") and voice recognition ("tell me what you want to do") systems, passing the cost of routing calls to the customer.

A corollary of the focus on transaction costs is management's belief that people (agents) need to be managed, controlled and motivated. Targets are set for agent activity (number of calls handled, time spent on calls etc.). Agent activity – adherence to targets – is used both to monitor agent behaviour (including the time taken in breaks) and as the basis for performance appraisal. First-level managers are taught to "coach" agents in pursuit of more productive activity. Agent teams are typically encouraged to compete for prizes and individual agents rewarded for "best" performance. A further feature of control is inspection; agents are inspected for conformance to prescriptions.

Service centres quickly earned the sobriquet "sweatshops", and it is not uncommon to see offices equipped with "fun" things like table football, table tennis, bean bags and so on, in an effort to ameliorate the misery. Not surprisingly, this provokes more cynicism than happiness, since the misery is caused not by lack of "fun" but by the way work is designed.

That, in summary, is the present style of management as applied to a simple service, the service centre. It is normal and ubiquitous, advocated by Big Consultancy and supported by a host of training and guidance services. The problem is that it doesn't work very well. The loud tell-tale signal – one that however remains inaudible to command-and-control mind-sets – is an inexorable rise in the volume of demand. It is what we call "failure demand", the amplitude of which is frequently astonishing.

Failure demand consists of *"demand caused by a failure to do something or do something right for the customer"**. It is a concept that is easily understood and easily misunderstood.

> *A civil servant working for the UK Cabinet Office heard about failure demand and found evidence that local authority services suffered high volumes of it. She sent an instruction for local authority managers to measure the extent of failure demand and set targets for its removal, ironically being unaware that target-setting is itself a major cause of failure demand...*

When the idea of failure demand is explained to command-and-control thinkers, they attribute it to a failure of people or processes to do the right things, exposing their mental models. They are wrong. Failure demand is systemic, that is, created by the system they have designed; an "improper design", to use Bower's language. It is a difficult conclusion for command-and-control managers to accept, since it requires them to acknowledge that everything they are doing is wrong. But before we explain why it is wrong – how these designs create such huge amounts of failure demand – here is an example of what is possible when organisations move beyond command and control.

> *In 2009 we worked with a financial services company whose leaders had decided to repatriate service operations from India (often called "onshoring"). They, like many others, had offshored operations primarily to lower costs and, perhaps, to follow fashion, as offshoring was widely touted by industry leaders and analysts as "best practice" at the time. At that period the organisation had about 200 customer service agents in the UK and about 500 in India. The motivation for the initiative was "customer retention", a tacit admission that poor service had been driving away customers in droves.*

---

* Seddon, J., (2003). *Freedom from Command and Control.* Buckingham: Vanguard Press

Naturally, managers had drawn up a plan, which concluded that repatriating the work would require another 500 seats in the UK. We suggested putting the plan on hold while we instead took the leaders out to study what was going on – in our language, to study the "what and why" of performance as a system.

Study quickly revealed that failure demand accounted for 70% of the total demand coming into the centre. The penny dropped: if we could design a service that worked for customers, the volume of demand – work to be done – would fall, effectively increasing the capacity of the operation. And this is what we did. We helped managers understand the causes of failure demand and design them out, resulting in a service that was effective for their customers. We will explain in more detail in the next chapter.

But the point to make here is that after the redesign and all the calls had been repatriated, it took only 300 UK agents to handle them. Leaders couldn't believe it: who would have imagined it to be possible? It was a seminal lesson that became renowned within the organisation, sparking curiosity among leaders as to how it was achieved. Today, with this philosophy embedded, the organisation describes the method as its customer service "signature".

This example raises many issues. Not least: who, faced with a brief to repatriate calls, would not have assumed that a plan would be required? When a service is redesigned for effectiveness it is safe to predict that capacity will increase – or the number of seats required will fall – but it is impossible to predict by how much. The extent of the improvement is "emergent": a consequence of the more effective design, which in turn is a consequence of changing managers' thinking about control and abandoning conventional service-centre practices in favour of better controls.

Before we expand on designing for effectiveness, we need to talk about the nature and means of this transformation – how leaders learn to go beyond command and control – for it is the route that is important. The route is the means to the end.

Summary:

Command-and-control management is normal and dysfunctional.

"Control" is the problem, rather than "command".

Controls in service centres focus on transaction cost, standardising and specialising work, and managing workers' activity. But managing costs drives costs up.

The signal of dysfunction is failure demand. Getting rid of it required a change to the system, the way work is designed and managed.

Change requires no plan.

The results speak for themselves.

2 The nature of the change

In chapter 1 we described a transformational change that required no plan – in fact it made the original plan redundant. This is unthinkable to command-and-control managers, for whom a plan for change including "deliverables", cost-benefit analyses and milestones, together with a programme and project management outline, is essential. When we inform leaders that none of these is necessary or even useful, they shake their heads, adamant in their insistence that starting out without a plan and benefits is impossible. When we stick to our guns, they often respond, "OK, so given your experience with similar companies, tell us what results we can expect here". But results will depend on what they, the leaders, actually do. If they treat this change as something to be delivered by their "improvement people", they will be heading for a train wreck, since those at the top won't have absorbed the philosophy that makes transformation possible. If, on the other hand, the leaders get hands-on, the change will very likely be rapid. But getting hands-on is not the way most leaders approach change. They expect to evaluate proposals and programmes in the abstract and at a distance. They don't expect to discover what the change process entails on the fly and in the thick of it – a radical and unnerving thought to a command-and-control thinker. Yet, counterintuitively, that's what is required.

We'll come back to the conventional command-and-control methods for planning change later. Let's start instead with a different example of how leaders react to counterintuitive truths.

Imagine that you stand up in a room full of leaders and suggest to them that targets are problematic. Their response will be to shake their heads and tell you that targets are fine so long as you choose the right target, or have the right people choose the target, or have people set their own targets. If you follow up by saying, no, the problem with targets is that they always make performance worse, they bristle. Some would say you're barmy; many would think it.

Few if any would respond positively or even with curiosity. When people brought up on command-and-control norms are exposed to an idea that runs counter to their deep beliefs, denial is a predictable reaction. Listeners can only map what is being said on to their current mind-set. If it challenges a fundamental belief, expect the recipient to deal with the dissonance in these ways.

Central to the Vanguard Method is a body of work called intervention theory. The purpose of the interventionist is to go into any system with the aims of fostering independence by showing incumbents how to acquire knowledge that will enable them to make informed choices on their own. This is unusual in the consulting world, where the big firms expect senior consultants to maintain a close enough relationship with the client that he or she does little or no independent thinking without them.

Key to intervention theory is the work of the US academic Chris Argyris,* an influential thinker in the field of organisation learning and development. To change a mental model requires, to use Argyris' expression, "double-loop learning", that is, questioning the assumptions behind one's beliefs. Single-loop learning, by contrast, is to repeat attempts at the same problem, for example trying to find better methods for setting a target. Double-loop learning is to change the mental model, to question assumptions – asking in this case, "why do we believe that targets are necessary for managing performance"?

As Argyris points out, challenging their beliefs makes leaders defensive ("there must be a right way to set a target"), and for this reason the Vanguard Method departs from his work in the way intervention is carried out. Experience has taught us that defensiveness dissolves when leaders see first-hand how their thinking (assumptions) governs performance. The distinction is between talking about assumptions and allowing their dysfunctional

---

* Argyris, C., (1970). *Intervention Theory and Method: A Behavioural Science View*, Addison Wesley

consequences to come to the surface as leaders directly study their system.

When we take managers into their organisation to study the "what and why" of current performance as a system, they can't avoid seeing exactly what targets and, for that matter, all other arbitrary measures sent down a hierarchy, do to performance. They are left in no doubt that they only serve to make it worse. It is impossible for them to ignore the dissonance created when they have seen it with their own eyes. When they discover that their supposed means of control are actually the reverse, they are forced to conclude that the control they afford is an illusion.

Vanguard was also influenced by the work of Chin and Benne*, who argued that there are three basic methods to effect change in human systems: rational, normative and coercive. Rational methods are exemplified by communication, training and the like – one party explains, the other listens. This book, by its nature, employs a "rational" approach. As we have seen, rational explanation runs the risk of turning off the unconverted by putting them on the defensive, which we try to defuse here by taking small steps and using practical examples. Normative methods are ways of taking action that deliberately aim to change norms, beliefs or attitudes. In our sphere, this means getting out into the organisation and studying how the work works at first hand. Experiencing a counterintuitive truth for yourself is quite different to reading it as words on a page. Straight denial is no longer an option. You are directly challenged to shift your mental model. Coercive strategies demand compliance through the use of sanctions, as, for example, in the case of UK public-sector reform and much of our approach to regulation. While coercive strategies can be useful as a tactic (there are times when leaders need to be bossy), as a means for transformation they are doomed to fail.

---

* Chin, R., and Benne, K.D., (1969). *General strategies for effecting changes in human systems* in Bennis, W.G., Benne, K.D., Chin, R., eds, *The Planning of Change* (2nd Edition) Holt, Rinehart and Winston Inc. USA

Rational strategies

The weakness of rational strategies is the tendency for the recipient to map what is communicated on to his or her current mental model ("but there must be a right way to set a target") rather than change it. Some – a very few – managers react constructively to rational strategies (being told), by becoming curious. Perhaps because they know in their hearts that something isn't right, or perhaps because they have witnessed the dysfunctional effects of command-and-control assumptions, their minds are at least partly open to re-thinking some fundamental beliefs.

But more usually, using rational strategies to challenge thinking provokes dissonance, with counterproductive consequences. If you doubt that, recall our examples of leaders leaving or being fired for talking our language, having had the audacity to point out the follies of command-and-control management in their organisation.

It is normal to see a schism in large organisations that have embarked on this kind of transformation. Because it is impossible to change the thinking of hundreds or thousands of managers at once, a point is reached where some have crossed the Rubicon while others are still on the further shore. Those who haven't tested the water react to what they hear (in "rational" mode) from the pioneers with incredulity, and, being human, they criticise, condemn and ridicule. In one organisation – a large financial services firm – we used what we called a "fundamentals programme" to begin the work of getting leaders curious. Those who hadn't yet been exposed to it called those who had "fundamentalists". Hearing, for example, that targets were being phased out, they translated it as meaning "no measures". What they imagined they heard was "fundamentalists" saying "let the people decide", and from that it was a small step to predicting anarchy.

For command-and-control managers (i.e. the majority), these are natural reactions – to which we respond, albeit perforce still in "rational" mode, as follows.

When we say "no targets", we mean that no arbitrary measures will be driven down the hierarchy for purposes of compliance. Instead, the measures-in-use – which are vital for understanding and improving performance – in the better design are all real / actual rather than arbitrary, and are derived from the purpose of the service in customer terms.

"Let the people decide" is something we would never say. The belief that that it is what is meant reflects the command-and-control mind-set that immediately suspects that decision-making has been removed from management. Addressing this issue, we would say something like: frontline workers not only can but should have the responsibility to make decisions relating to their work: the measures-in-use giving them direct line of sight to purpose in customer terms and how well it is being achieved, they are better placed than anyone else to understand and improve performance. As you will see later, this is a profoundly better form of control – which then requires a complementary change in the role and functions of management.

In the same vein, people who have yet to be involved in an intervention can find the language used off-putting; for instance, "the customer's nominal value" may sound like impenetrable jargon. In fact, it's a non-ambiguous way of summing up the performance of our perfect service centre – it consists of exactly what they need to be satisfied, nothing more, nothing less. It is part of a new language representing a novel and important focus for management.

Another jarring phrase for many is "roll-in". "Why on earth can't they use roll-out like everyone else?" people complain. But there are important distinctions between the two. In essence, roll out is, "here is the answer, now do it" – a classical command-and-control approach to executing change. Roll-in on the other hand is a normative process that takes people out of a conventional command-and-control design, helps them understand clearly what the design faults were and how these affected their jobs, clarifies the purpose of their new role, provides them with the appropriate training to do their work and trains them in the use of new measures for controlling and improving what they are doing. Roll-in is re-educational; normative.

The Vanguard Method is normative; unusually it starts with study, or gaining knowledge. Study always reveals shocking instances of performance failure and blind spots that were previously hidden from view. Explaining such things to "outsiders" not involved in their discovery often provokes denial and/or objections that the examples are unrepresentative, cherry-picked, or plain wrong. "Insiders" can be vilified ("fundamentalists") or labelled arrogant for being critical of management.

These are natural human consequences associated with discovering and communicating truths that contradict the conventional wisdom. In the course of this book we will expose many such counterintuitive truths; as we illustrate them and discuss the better alternatives all will, we hope, become clear. The important point to note here is that, as large organisations go through the change process, divisions of views will surface that can become destructive and dysfunctional unless measures are taken to counteract or diminish them.

> *The marketing director of an insurance organisation was horrified to learn that following a transformation that led to sales growth of 30% the "share of wallet" – measuring the proportion of customers buying multiple products – had shrunk, along with her bonus that was dependent on it. She was insistent on reversing the design change. But study had shown that customers hated the cross-selling that "share of wallet" implied, which involved selling them products that they didn't want or need (which in addition caused substantial failure demand downstream). The chief executive stepped in to stop any reversion.*

There are times when leaders need to be bossy.

Normative strategies

Normative strategies intentionally create double-loop learning – re-thinking assumptions behind the things we do as leaders, ultimately altering our mental models. To put it simply, the best way to start the journey beyond command and control, and achieving substantial, some would say radical change, is to study. When they study the "what and why" of current performance as a system, leaders find themselves confronted with a series of unpalatable truths. It makes their heads hurt – after all, they are discovering that much of what they believed about management is wrong – but it also generates enormous energy for constructive change. When that energy is put to use creating a better design, and that design demonstrably produces far superior results, managers can't go back. For them, command and control is dead.

To illustrate how study illuminates, we return to our simple service centre. To recap: we have already described how studying demand reveals that much of it is systemic, created by the system itself: it is failure demand. Failure demand can't be turned off by blaming people or procedures ("if only they did as they should"). The only way to eradicate it is to design a system that works effectively for the customer. But the starting point for the redesign is the impetus generated by understanding what actually causes failure demand – which, perhaps surprisingly, it is every feature of the command-and-control model.

Paradoxically, to understand what goes wrong, leaders first need to work out what right looks like. That means studying value demands – the things customers want that the service centre exists to serve – and define for each the value work, that which has to be done precisely to give customers what they want (or meet their nominal value). When they are clear on that, leaders study what happens as value demands pass through their system.

In the case of our service centre, leaders quickly get that limiting call times and standardising work (as with set scripts) both hinder the system from responding to the variety of customer demands, creating failure demand. They also get that specialising the work increases the number of handovers, which increases errors and the time customer demands spend in the system, again generating failure demand. They see that setting targets for activities focuses the agents' minds on meeting the targets rather than on serving customers (compare with "teaching to the test" in schools). They discover to their horror that the people they thought were their "best" agents are actually those who are cleverest at using their ingenuity to game the system, win prizes or avoid punishment. They learn that the major causes of variation in the time agents take to satisfy customer needs are natural to the system and have nothing to do with the agent (more on how to prove this later), bringing their whole approach to "people management" in question; and they also discover that inspecting agents' performance drives them to comply with the requirements of inspectors rather than those of customers. When they think about the purpose of the service centre from the customers' point of view, they can see that far too few customer demands are met at the first point of transaction. With the veil lifted, the causes of failure demand are suddenly clear. Seeing that they are all systemic, leaders understand that it is the design that is the problem, and they can accept the counterintuitive truth that by chasing efficiency (managing costs) they have undermined effectiveness (and driven up costs).

To return to the repatriation of service work from India:

> *As is common, the outsource organisation worked to service-level agreements and average handling times. Mystery shopping and "quality sampling" (inspection) were used to control service agents' behaviour. As is also common with offshoring relationships, there was a detailed description of respective roles, leading to arguments about adherence to the contract (where work should be done and whether it had been done as agreed) and constant communications between a large number of people in "escalation" roles who were progress-chasing issues. The contract was the most insidious*

cause of failure demand. With the supplier working strictly to the detailed specifications, it was quickly clear that the latter were preventing agents from meeting any variety in customer demand, instead frequently returning the work to the UK. As a result, customers were being shuffled between onshore and offshore agents, in extremis experiencing as many as 17 transactions to get what they wanted. On average, leaders learned, one customer demand would lead to two-and-a-half transactions. No wonder customers were unhappy.

Two important and complementary types of learning occur as leaders study. They have to unlearn before they can learn. They understand that it is the system – the way work is designed and managed – that is the cause of sub-optimal performance; but also, and more importantly, they have begun the process of absorbing the things they will need to fully understand in order to design a more effective service. Top of the list are knowledge of customer demand, appreciation of what constitutes the value work (what matters to customers) and understanding how to measure the system's achievement of purpose in customer terms. These, as we shall illustrate shortly, are crucial elements of the future design.

The "back office"

It's time to move beyond the simple service centre. In the early days of service centres, and perhaps exacerbated by the problem of rising demand, leaders were faced with a dilemma. When agents finish a customer call, there is a "wrap time" as they sign off and complete the transaction. During this time they are either unavailable to take the next call, with the risk that the centre's agreed "service level" (eg, picking up the call within four rings) will be breached, or they take the call and interrupt themselves, breaking their concentration and possibly failing to complete the previous transaction later.

A certain Richard Chase* came up with a "solution". Recognising that management's preoccupation was to sweat the labour – maximise the productivity of the agents – Chase proposed to overcome the dilemma by "de-coupling" the customer from the service. While the service centre would find out what the customer wanted, the actual work would be sent to a back office, free from customer contact, where management would be free to concentrate on maximising productivity. The "back office" was born.

We should note that the term "back office" is now routinely applied to a different idea, the centralisation of support services like HR, IT and finance, sometimes called shared services or economies of scale. We discuss this idea later.

Back offices are designed in much the same way as service centres, with a focus on activity management, standardisation, specialisation and the cost of transactions. When leaders study the "what and why" of back-office performance, they find exactly the same things as they do in service centres – standardisation preventing the system absorbing the variety of customer demand; specialisation increasing handovers, work activity and mistakes; activity targets creating a focus on the activity at the expense of achievement of purpose – with the addition of a new feature, the separation of "front" and "back" offices that creates two different views of the customer, the latter driven by rules, the former including the customer and their context. All of these features – we call them system conditions – generate failure demand. The "back office", created on the basis of the need to sweat the labour, just adds to the problem. In short, studying reveals a simple, inescapable fact: the command-and-control design doesn't work. As Deming would say, it leads to sub-optimisation, i.e. poorer performance than is possible if we thought about it in a more sensible way.

To see first-hand how this industrial (front-office / back-office)

---

* Chase, R.B., (1978). *Where does the customer fit in a service operation?* Harvard Business Review, Vol. 56 No. 4, pp. 137-42

design undermined performance in our financial services example, we had leaders follow value demands through their system. They took demands where customers wanted to buy a product, with instructions to follow the work from beginning to an end point where the customer received something, and ask: is this "clean" from the customer's point of view, i.e. can we be confident this will not create failure demand?

The first case each took failed the test. The usual reaction of the leaders was to point to the case being "unusual". So we asked them to take another, and another, and another, and they soon had to acknowledge that very little travelled through cleanly.They found that one demand ("I want to buy a product") could be turned into as many as nine separate tasks and sent off to respective back-offices. They could see that their working assumptions were that these parts of the work would arrive in the right places, where people would have the necessary skills, would do the work in the standard times and would return it completed within the service-level agreements.

As Deming put it: Pleasant dreams!

"The supposition is prevalent the world over that there would be no problems in production or in service if only our production workers would do their jobs in the way that they were taught. Pleasant dreams. The workers are handicapped by the system, and the system belongs to management." *

Designing for effectiveness

And so we return to our perfect service centre, a workplace that serves customers by giving them precisely what they need. A place that has no back office and none of the normal features associated with command-and-control service designs. It is the new design that led to the profound improvement in performance – much

---

* Deming, W.E., (1982). *Out of the Crisis*. MIT Press: Massachusetts

better customer service at much lower costs, with highly motivated service agents working in concert with managers who now have complementary roles. As we describe designing for effectiveness you may – if you are not in the service-centre industry – wonder why all service centres don't work in this sensible way. But as we shall illustrate, the design cuts across current command-and-control beliefs.

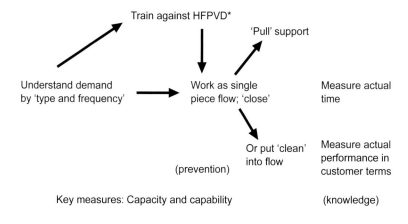

*HFPVD = High Frequency Predictable Value Demand

The effective service design archetype

The critical lever is understanding demand in customer terms. You may wonder, as Peter Day did when he interviewed one of us,* why leaders of service organisations don't have knowledge of customer demand – that is to say, an understanding of what customers want from the service. To the extent that they do, it is based on volumes, for, as we explained, the command-and-control thinker worries about the volume of calls, how long people take to deal with them and how many people they have. The fact that few command-and-control managers even know about the existence of failure demand is indicative.

---

* www.bbc.co.uk/radio4/news/inbusiness/inbusiness_20070104.shtml

The key to effective design is to understand customers' value demands – the things they need from the service, in their terms. Understanding the type, frequency and predictability of value demands enables organisations to train the service agents to deal with customers' needs. It is common to learn through studying demand that much of it is predictable ("give me this or that") and it is these predictable demands that become the focus for service-agent training. In many organisations this cuts the training period from as much as eight weeks to two. Agents begin work confident that these are the types of call they will receive most of, and that they can handle them. When an agent gets a call they are not trained to deal with, they do not pass it on – instead they "pull" help from experts. Because demand analysis has taught managers what to expect, they can place experts on hand to teach agents how to handle calls they are not yet trained to do.

The agents are no longer constrained by time limits for handling calls; instead the actual time taken is measured. When agents begin, and as and when they learn to handle more demands, they will take longer; as they learn, they do things more quickly. Knowledge of actual time taken thus improves resource planning – how many people are needed to handle the work.

One key measure of performance is the proportion of calls handled on the first transaction – after all, that's what customers want. In many service centres, calls cannot be handled at the first point of transaction because the service requires something else to happen, for example sending out an engineer, police officer or health worker to provide a face-to-face service. With these calls the focus for leaders and agents is whether the customer demands sent through to the frontline workers are "clean"– in other words, giving the recipient exactly what they need to carry out their job. And for a service that can only meet customers' needs when a task is passed on, the measure in use is related to the purpose of the service from the customers' point of view, for example home repairs completed on the day and time the customer wants; first pension payments on the day they are due. Two key measures for the organisation are capacity – the volume of demands we can service – and capability – how well we do them, measured in terms that matter to customers (timeliness, right-first-time). Finally, this archetype is designed according to the principle of prevention; quality theory teaches us it is better to prevent errors rather than inspect for them. We return to this distinction in chapter 12.

You will recognise the archetype described above in all of the examples we present in this book.

Now consider the impact of this design on morale: The agent has moved from a world where adherence to activity targets (calls per day, service levels), scripts, protocols and the like was the norm – where that created tension between meeting requirements and serving customers – to a world where they are confidently equipped – and trusted – to serve customers and learn to solve more problems for customers every day. Their first-level manager has moved away from monitoring agents' activity and instead is focused on how to help each agent handle more customer demands. The culture change is palpable; it is a joy to go to work! Culture – the way people behave – is a product of the system. The system is now designed for perfect – although perfect is rarely attainable, that is the aim – and, being effective at delivering service, failure demand is eradicated quickly, increasing capacity. Seeing it in action, managers learn another profound lesson: culture change comes free.

> *To return to our example of repatriating calls from India: We helped the leaders set up an "on-shoring" team who, with a clear customer-centric purpose, would work to learn what was required to give nothing short of amazing customer service. The focus was on learning how to make work completely "clean" – perfect for the customer – and in the early stages no attention was paid to the time it took. The priority was learning, not production.*
>
> *Within six weeks, leaders had a good understanding of customer "value" demands, their frequency and predictability.*

Knowledge of the value demands enabled the team to build the necessary expertise to serve customers confidently and well, and as the team developed, more service agents were "rolled in" to the new way of working.

If you don't work in a service centre, you'll find all of the above quite sensible. If you do, you'll be likely to find everything about it challenging and, going back to the point about "rational" attempts to change, you'll probably have objections. If we stood in a room, presented the design archetype above, and explained to command-and-control managers that this is a more effective way to design a service centre, many would think we are barmy. Here are some of the common objections:

"You can't train people in two weeks"

The usual training focuses on procedures, inspection protocols, products, navigating IT systems, and so on. Training revisited focuses on understanding and meeting what customers need to fulfil the (predictably) most frequent demands. As a result, agents are full of confidence as opposed to the usual fear of going live after many weeks of organisationally-focused rather than customer-focused training.

"Agents can't do everything"

This is the rationale for agents in conventionally managed organisations to be specialised, which also – to a command-and-control thinker – cuts training costs. But until you study demand from the customers' point of view, and understand what they actually want, by definition you can't know how much agents can do. When managers do know these things and embark on training against demand, they are always amazed at how much – predictably – agents can accomplish.

"They'll take too long"

Command-and-control managers think measuring actual time taken to handle calls is madness. Controlling activity time is central to their ideas about control; they imagine that left to themselves agents will take it easy, take longer than required; in short, take the mickey. But they don't. Agents have moved from a world where their manager focuses on activity, paying attention to them when the statistics don't fit the plan – an adversarial relationship – to a world where they work every day not only to solve customer problems but also, with management's help, to learn to solve more of them – a relationship of common purpose. The measures-in-use help both the agent and manager to work on improving the service.

"Costs can only go up"

Command-and-control managers imagine costs will rise because their whole approach to costs (and budgeting) is focused on activity times; controlling activity time is the fundamental platform for management. But as they cross the Rubicon they learn that cost is not in individual transactions but end-to-end; it is the total number of transactions it takes customers to get a service. As effectiveness increases the immediate impact is a dramatic fall in failure demand (and the cost associated with it), increasing capacity. They learn that cost is a "lagging" measure. As effectiveness – achievement of purpose in customer terms, a "leading" measure – improves, costs fall.

"Removing inspection will mean more errors"

What managers fail to appreciate is that inspection, however strict, does nothing to reduce errors. Being another counterintuitive truth, it is something they may have to study to believe – you can't improve with inspection. The vast majority of errors are created by the system, not agents (we'll show you exercises to establish this and other truths in chapter 12). The better design places emphasis on prevention rather than inspection: agents are trained with a focus on customer demand, have responsibility to do good work and can pull on help as required. Their supervisors are focused on the same end, making supervision a closer, more collaborative relationship.

A better role for management

In conventional command-and-control service centres, managers are preoccupied with cost and activity management; as we have shown, that is part of the problem. In this more effective design managers have more productive roles. Think about the archetype diagram and consider what might need "managing" in this system.

- Is demand changing? How should that inform the way we train agents?
- Can we do more to ensure more customers get their issue resolved at the first point of transaction?
- When expertise is "pulled" does it arrive quickly? Should the expertise be designed to be "pulled" offline, or does demand dictate it be built into the front line?
- When work has to be passed to another person or function for service delivery, does it travel "clean"? How well is this working end-to-end?

These better activities for managers ensure they are working on the system. They are the basis for designing management roles. Further, once a more effective design is established, management's attention is drawn to the way support functions (IT, HR, finance) operate. The focus is: given we now have a more effective service design, to what extent does any support function actually create value for or impede operations?

We'll return to support functions in Part 2. What we've established in this chapter is the nature of this change – changing thinking – and the means; studying, understanding the "what and why" of performance as a system. While we have focused on a relatively simple service – the service centre – the same principles apply to more complex service systems.

Summary

The problems managers think they have are not the real problems; the real problems are revealed through study. Study is essential because it is normative; it challenges mental models and provides more constructive ones to put in their place. Through it leaders learn that their central problem is command-and-control thinking.

The major revelation of studying is that conventional command-and-control "controls" actually force the system out of control. Command-and-control management has, as its primary focus, the management of costs. Chasing efficiency through standardisation, specialisation and activity management drives costs up. Managing costs causes costs.

The better model is to "design against demand": focus on what creates value for customers in their terms and measure achievement of purpose in customer terms. These are to work on effectiveness, not efficiency. These new controls maintain a clear focus on perfection and provide the means to track progress. Managing value leads to a fall in costs and a rise in capacity.

Organisational sustainability and agility are secured, as the lodestar for design is customer demand.

Before we continue to further examples of studying and designing services we must open the discussion on the most pernicious system condition lying behind command-and-control thinkers' focus on efficiency: budget management.

3 Budget management

Budget management, you will recall, was an idea developed by an accountant, James McKinsey, and was seized on by big-company managers as a framework for bringing large, multi-business corporations under control a century ago. Today, McKinsey's invention is the lynchpin of command-and-control management – its structure of control.

Top management uses the budget to allocate financial resources to divisions or departments of the organisation. They report to finance managers whose job is to hold the parts to budgeted plans and revise the latter in the case of variance. Spending and, where relevant, revenue, are kept under constant review. On the face of it, this seems sensible. Operational leaders shouldn't be able to spend monies willy-nilly, any more than their units should stray wildly over or under budget, both of which would seem to indicate that the organisation was out of control.

But how much of the copious effort involved in setting budgets, discussing variance and wrestling the bureaucracy to revise budgets or modify the organisation to stay "on budget", is of any value to the enterprise? How much of it is productive, instructive, or even based on knowledge?

The disaffection with budget management has been well documented by the Beyond Budgeting Round Table (BBRT)*. In surveys, senior finance leaders say that improvement and reform of budget management is a top priority. Former GE CEO Jack Welch called budgeting "the bane of corporate America. It never should have existed." Among the problems commonly cited:

Rhythm: Strategic intent is long term, budget management is short term; monthly requirements to be on budget are inconsistent with changes in circumstances.

---

* www.bbrt.org

Resource consumption: Budgeting consumes an enormous amount of time and effort on the part of finance and operational people; agreeing, reviewing, reconciling, justifying and defending budget numbers.

Gaming: Engaging operational leaders' ingenuity in: ensuring improvements are modest rather than challenging; making the numbers regardless of the impact on the organisation; moving revenues and costs forward or backwards to suit the budget and dis-incentivising profound improvement.

Validity: Forecasts and associated budgets are guesses and only right by chance; it is impossible to predict financial performance accurately.

Illusory: Budget management is an illusion of control.

While these concerns are not new and widely shared, budgeting endures as a tedious corporate ritual. Despite the dysfunction, budget management is seen as both necessary and unavoidable – evidence of a deep-rooted conviction that there is no alternative. It is after all the central means of corporate control. What is lacking is an understanding of better ones.

Most of the common concerns are symptoms, the last – budget management as an illusion of control – being the most important and insidious. As we demonstrate with examples in this book, managers striving to hit arbitrary numbers drive costs up, service quality down, and systems into instability. Because it employs arbitrary measures that are not based in knowledge of how the operations use or generate money, budget management makes performance worse. It is not just an ineffective form of control; it draws a veil over the means for improvement and competes with real controls. Worse than an illusion of control, it actually drives the system into disorder.

Fundamental to the control of organisations is knowledge of how operations use and generate money. That may seem an obvious truth, and operational and finance managers often understandably react strongly to the suggestion that they lack such knowledge. They point to how money has been used, for example, in different parts of the operations, assuming that this is "knowledge". But they do not know if that money needed to be spent, if it created value for customers, or if it was used effectively in non-customer-facing functions. When we at Vanguard think of "how" money is spent, we distinguish between what is spent in creating value for customers (doing the value work and only that) and what is used for other (many) non-value activities. Thinking this way and working out how money is actually consumed is an extraordinary eye-opener for leaders – another counterintuitive experience. As a measure, this is actual, not arbitrary, and genuinely instructive. It informs rather than constrains. We'll concentrate on how service organisations use money in this and the next chapters.

But a brief word on how organisations generate money. This was covered more fully in *Freedom from Command and Control.** The gist of the argument is as follows. How often do you hear leaders say, "Half of my marketing budget works, but I don't know which half"? Of course he (usually a he) doesn't know what the real amount is: it might be half, it might be more. At Vanguard, what we want to know is how many customer acquisition processes a company has. This might seem a strange question. But customers come in through a variety of processes, and when you have a handle on what they are and how well or badly they work, you are in a position to bring customers in more effectively – and turn off sales and marketing initiatives that don't, thus saving money as well.

At this point, we will return to the conventional service centre / back office design to illustrate how budget management works. We will relate that to what we have already discussed about the realities of operational performance, firstly demonstrating the ways budget

---

* Seddon, J., (2003). *Freedom from Command and Control.*
Buckingham: Vanguard Press

management locks in the status quo and then considering budget management's role in a more effective service design.

How budget management works

Transactions and transaction costs form the basis for budget management in service centres. To formulate the budget, managers forecast volumes of expected transactions on the basis of historic data on call volumes and other non-telephone activities. They then calculate anticipated time needed to handle the work from current activity times for the various activities in the front and back offices. This translates into the required headcount, with adjustments made for absence and training. (Absence, a symptom of low morale, tends to be high in command-and-control designs.) The ratio of team leaders to agents is set – typically between six and 18 agents per team leader – and that gives us the basic components of the budget, which can subsequently be broken down into activity targets or KPIs for the levels down the organisation.

The alert reader may have noted that budget management takes no account the phenomenon of failure demand. Current volumes of demand are enshrined in the budgeting process without differentiation, with no understanding of the cost and diminished capacity that is thereby internalised. Further, the emphases on transaction costs, headcount and absence mean what ought to be thought of as a dynamic system is frozen as is – as static as it is ineffective.

The effects of budget management

The first effect to note is the problem described above: in treating all demand as "work to be done", volumes of failure demand are permanently embedded in the system – a giant cuckoo in the nest greedily consuming capacity and effort. To remind you what we are talking about here: in financial services failure demand frequently runs between 40% and 70% of the total, in utilities and public services 90% or even more.

Basing the budget on transaction costs has the consequences already noted. If budgets are overspent, managers either plead for more resources (people) or bear down on transaction times or agent costs (the latter by moving calls to lower-wage providers). Another response is to "migrate" customer calls to digital channels, the internet or voice-recognition systems. Typically this creates yet more failure demand (we explain why when we discuss digital services later), so while targets for shifting customers to digital may be met, the budget in face-to-face or telephone services rises inexorably.

Unfortunately, there is no positive effect discernible from budget management. You can be "on budget" and still have large unknown, unnecessary costs.

Different thinking about control

Before we consider changing the budgeting process, we have to think about better means of control. Three things matter, and they have been introduced already:

- Demand
- Value work
- Achievement of purpose in customer terms

If we understand demand in customer terms – and now we are talking about value demands, what customers want from us – we can begin to work on equipping frontline workers with the knowhow they need to serve customers: the starting-place for our perfect service centre.

As we discussed earlier, studying customer demand always reveals that, counter to most managers' beliefs, it is extremely predictable. Once managers appreciate the predictability of demand and use it to provide staff with the necessary expertise to handle it (ensuring that support is available as needed on a "pull" basis to teach them how to handle demands for which they are not yet trained), their focus can turn to the important topic of the use their system of service makes of money. Moreover, in so doing they learn how to distinguish the good use of money (doing value work) from the not-good (everything else).

As we illustrated, the old command-and-control measure of adherence to activity times (an arbitrary measure) is abandoned in favour of measuring the actual time taken. There is a good reason for this. Because customer demands – and types – vary, the time taken to meet them will not be the same. The measure of activity is now no longer static but dynamic, no longer used to manage agents but instead to achieve more reliable resource planning – if people reliably take "x" amount of time to meet predictable demand, how many people on seats will we need? Have no doubt that cutting the link between resource-planning metrics and the way people work is a significant break with command-and-control convention.

Consequences for financial results

The first and most compelling consequence of designing services against demand is that the volume of failure demand falls, often dramatically. The effect of reducing failure demand is to expand the system's capacity. What's more, as service agents learn to give customers exactly what they (predictably) need, the costs of service fall too. When they see the service consistently coming in under budget, period by period, leaders understand that managing to a budget is unnecessary. Budget management can be seen for what it is – a part of the problem and an impediment to finding a better solution. Leaders gain first-hand knowledge of how the original promise of order in fact creates disorder. The rapid fall in operating expenses exposes the costs of the disorder and diminishes the perceived value of conventional management accounting, posing a big question over the purpose of budget management.

Once stable, the new design gives an accurate measure of the true (lower) cost of effective service, which can then be used with confidence to predict future operating costs. Operating costs are treated as a "lagging" measure – a consequence of working with the new controls ("leading" measures). There will always be a relationship between demand and capacity, and it will be clearer than ever it could have been previously. We'll give an example of this in the next chapter. The question to be asked here is: if we can predict costs, is there any point in conventional budget management?

Re-thinking budget management is a consequence of achieving a more effective service design, an effect, not the starting-place. Knowledge of how the system uses and creates money has to come first.

The next two chapters will expand on these ideas with examples.

4 Break-fix systems

To illustrate the folly of command-and-control thinking and, in particular, budget management, in this chapter we move on from the simple service centre to a more complex type of service: what we call "break-fix" systems. Break-fix systems do what the name suggests – they are for mending broken buildings, computers, infrastructure, health and many other things. No apologies for focusing here on housing repairs and in the next chapter on people whose lives have fallen off the rails: while they may be familiar to some readers, for new ones they graphically illustrate a number of quite complex issues that arise in managing services businesses, from scheduling, resource and materials management, to multi-agency working and how to handle with confidence the infinite variety of demands emanating from the human condition. Although they are different in terms of their task or mission, they share the same archetype; both are systems whose purpose is to take remedial action – something is "broken" and needs to be "fixed".

Public housing repairs services are typically designed in the following way: the customer in need of a repair calls a service centre which records the demand and creates a specification for what is to be done, often with an associated target time or service level for the response. The specification is passed to a specialist (in this case the appropriate tradesperson) who will attend and carry out the repair.

It is an example we often use with senior finance people when we want to open their eyes to the problems of budget management – housing repairs are something everyone can relate to. We present them with budget information, the usual lines of budget numbers, actuals and variances for a repairs organisation. The largest budget items are personnel and material costs. We tell them their challenge is to reduce costs without having any adverse effect on service quality – or, if they can, even improve it.

At this point, finance managers whip out their pencils and eagerly focus on the big numbers – the assumption being that the easiest way to make savings is cut people and/or material costs. Discussions ensue about how to increase the productivity of repair and service-centre workers (respectively, raise the number of jobs per day, and reduce call times or replace agents with an "app") in order to cut headcount. To bring down the cost of materials, they typically focus on tactics to reduce unit costs (buy from cheaper suppliers or in bulk) or limit materials in use by only buying them when required or by adding paperwork to make access more difficult. They sometimes go on to the smaller numbers: whether to service vehicles less frequently, route tradespeople to cut down travel time and cost, and the like.

When they have presented their ideas (none of which, by the way, will get anywhere near their goal), we help them see the wider context of performance management and how that is connected to the budget. The budget is only one of – albeit central to – the means of control. Managers in the service centre will be concentrated on the usual service-centre metrics – service level (picking up the phone), activity times (how long agents take on calls) and compliance with the process (completing the paperwork); managers of repair personnel will be homing in on jobs-per-tradesperson-per-day, meeting target times for repairs, and material costs.

So here we have the full array of conventional command-and-control controls. We're going to explain what those "controls" actually do to performance (you guessed: they make it worse than it ought to be). But before we do, here is a teaser. Repairs services that have gone beyond command and control routinely deliver repairs on the day and at the time customers specify – and do so at strikingly lower cost than before. Imagine the economic impact if all such services did that!

Our first foray into housing repairs took place in 2002. We had plenty of experience in IT support services and utilities maintenance, but housing repairs was a new area for us. The assignment started well.

We applied the method – more on what that looks like shortly – the result of which was to free up capacity to carry out more repairs with the same resources. Unfortunately, since the organisation's housing stock was in poor condition, the effect of the capacity boost was to increase spending on materials. When the service went over budget, the operations director pulled the plug. On the plus side, we now knew how housing repairs functioned as a system and could use what we'd learned to help others apply it.

Other organisations with poor-quality stock experienced the same period of rising materials costs as a consequence of increasing capacity as our guinea-pig. But when they stuck to their guns through that initial phase, they made some remarkable discoveries. It wasn't just that total demand began to fall as the quality of the housing stock improved. At the same time, the morale of tenants went up, as did their regard for their local authority – and, something no one had expected, they began to take greater responsibility for their environment as their pride in it grew. In other words, better service generates engagement: improvement is reciprocal.

In our early interventions in housing repairs, we helped leaders to measure and focus on end-to-end times for completing repairs, as opposed to targets. But as our understanding grew, one of our colleagues, John Little, developed a way of working in which repairs could be carried out on the day and at the time the tenant requested. The first to achieve this was a local authority*. Imagine… if your utility companies could do that, your first reaction would be disbelief; then you'd cheer.

The route the leaders took and the results that followed are within the grasp of any leader of a system that follows the break-fix pattern. So, if, as is likely, you are working in an area different from housing repairs or what we call people-centred services (next chapter), read on and think about the principles rather than the nitty-gritty.

---

* https://vanguard-method.net/2014/10/housing/

To recap: getting beyond command and control begins with study – leaders won't give up their current controls until they have witnessed first-hand how they destabilise and send the system out of control. At the same time, as part of studying how well, or poorly, the system performs from a different point of view, leaders develop new measures. As they do so, they begin to see how changing the design of work will enable these measures to be both a better means of control and an important factor in understanding performance and identifying ways to improve it.

Following demand in the service centre typically reveals that 50% or more consists of failure demand. If service levels (picking up the phone in x rings) and activity targets are being met and overall repair times are on target, this causes something of a puzzle. Why are customers unhappy when our controls are telling us that all systems are go?

Next, leaders might go out with repair personnel to answer a simple but previously unasked question: how often do we complete the repair on the first visit, and, if not, why not? They discover that, typically, fewer than 40% of repairs are completed on the first call. This is a shock: their most important resource, the people who deliver on the purpose of the service, are dramatically unproductive. What if they could carry out every repair every time they turned up, how much capacity would that release? How can it be that we complete so few, yet are still meeting the targets? The mystery deepens. Often leaders get a second shock, the reports they have been receiving on "first-time fix" are nothing like the reality and they begin to see how the measure is gamed.

When they address the second question – why couldn't we fix it? – leaders find they have opened a can of worms. Repairs aren't completed at the first call because tradespeople don't have the right materials, the time allocated is insufficient, the customer is not in, and/or the real job is different from the one specified on the ticket. Delving into the detail explains in shocking clarity how management signals can tell them service is excellent at the same time as customers are filling the service centre with failure demand. When the tradesperson fails to complete for one of the reasons above, the case is typically logged as closed and the customer requested to call in to open a new ticket and arrange a fresh visit. Many jobs require a series of activities carried out by different tradespeople, each with its own target time, so the same job (from the customer's angle) can require multiple tickets and multiple transactions with the service centre. So long as the tradesperson turns up during the specified time bracket – a morning or an afternoon, sometimes a day – he has met his target, while the elapsed time experienced by the customer stretches to weeks or months. Some jobs are partially completed, opening further job tickets. Tradespeople spend time buying or withdrawing materials from stores, a perfectly unproductive use of a productive resource, especially as materials supply procedures are often time-consuming and bureaucratic. This is a system that is literally out of control – how could it be otherwise when the measures managers use give them no information about its real performance to the end customer?

When they take a step back and consider how far short their operation falls of the purpose of the system from the customer's point of view ("turn up when it suits me and fix it"), managers realise that they have created an absurd system: how can two non-specialist parties – customer and service-centre agent – be expected to accurately specify what the expert repair person needs to do the job perfectly, every time? Also clear is the dysfunction created by their supposed "controls" all through the service; it is the system that is the problem and that has to change.

While everything might be "green" on the RAG (Red, Amber, Green) status, study reveals that "green" doesn't mean green; it actually means red. Managers learn that their service is ineffective – it fails to achieve its purpose. To design an effective system requires changing the means of control, so we return to the three essential means of control: demand, value work and achievement of purpose.

In all transactional services, the big performance lever is demand. How predictable is demand? If you ask managers of break-fix systems that question, if they have thought about it at all, they will reply that demand can't be predicted. Yet study shows the opposite: over time the overall volume of work to be done is largely predictable. Digging down to major repair types reveals that here too volumes are mostly predictable. This is precious knowledge, since it enables leaders to make two other important predictions: they can identify the expertise required by tradespeople to do the most frequent jobs, and the materials that they will require to carry them out. In other words, knowledge of demand dictates the value work – the expertise and materials required.

Analysis of historical data on materials used in repairs allows leaders to gauge the rate of consumption. That, together with knowledge of supplier cycle times – how quickly they can deliver – leads to an altogether different approach to control of materials. Instead of agonising over material costs, leaders focus on the time materials spend in their system. They come to see that purchasing materials at the rate of use or consumption leads to lower material costs overall – a major counterintuitive truth.

The design of an effective repairs service follows the archetype introduced in chapter 2. The service centre's task is restricted to establishing when the tenant wants a job carried out and allocating a time to turn up and do it – something that is now possible because leaders know the real capacity (number of jobs they can reliably do) of their system. Removing job specification from the service centre recognises that accurate diagnosis can only be made by the tradesman in front of the problem. When he/she arrives at the job, the tradesperson informs central controllers how long the work will take – essential for estimating when he/she will be free for the next one. While knowledge of demand will ensure that tradespeople carry all the most frequently used materials – increasing the capability to complete on first visit – there will always be occasions when non-standard items are needed. In those cases, the tradesperson calls up the materials from central controllers who time delivery for the appropriate juncture: the best time to receive a new bath is when the old one has been removed, for example. These are the basic features of an effective design.

To return to our discussion of the nature of this change in chapter 2, consider the likely reaction of a command-and-control thinker to a presentation of these features as the "solution" to his or her issues, without having scrutinised their system at first-hand first. All of them would be challenging in the extreme. Ask the tenants when they want it done? Let tradesmen decide how long they will need? Provide materials as and when tradesmen ask for them? For command-and-control thinkers, such outlandish ideas would be dismissed out of hand as a surrender of control. In reality they are essential for bringing organisations under true as opposed to fake control, via knowledge of demand, what constitutes value work, and how well customer purpose is being achieved. To illustrate how this works in practice, here's an example:

Martin, the leader of a housing repairs service, solved the scheduling problem and dissolved the budget-management problem. His journey beyond command and control began in 2010 when he and his team set out to study their system. Using time-series data, they learned that the volume of demand was predictable, showing a horseshoe pattern; demand rose in winter. Analysis found repeatable patterns for all major repair types. Bricklaying showed a "reverse" horseshoe, rising in summer rather than winter months, but, as in all other major cases, volumes were predictable.

To provide a system capable of delivering service as and when tenants require, sufficient resources in the shape of tradespeople must be available. Martin's team next worked out the median time taken for each of the most important types of repair, adding 15% to ensure sufficient capacity, the principle being that you need to ensure you have sufficient resource to match the demand. To maximise workforce flexibility, tradespeople were given basic training in other associated trades. For example, while a plasterer is needed to plaster a wall, other trades can learn how to fill in cracks. This principle was applied to all trades other than electrical and gas repairs, which are necessarily regulated for safety (although the other way round, electricians and gas engineers were perfectly capable of learning the basic techniques of companion trades). These steps solved the problem of scheduling, ensuring the system had the capacity required to service the demand.

As a result of this redesign, the value of materials held in stock fell by half, while repairs completed requiring only van stock – something not measured under the old system – was above 80%. Arriving to do repairs within 30 minutes of the scheduled time – again, not something even countenanced under the old system – was at the same level. The volume of calls to the service centre dropped by half as a consequence of an effective system removing failure demand, and the time taken on calls by a similar amount. In short, better service at much lower cost, achieved by focusing on effectiveness.

The further consequence was a dissolving of the budget-management problem. In the first year of the new system, Martin's operation came in under budget, which had been established by using historic cost. The same happened for four years in a row, for each of which historic costs, which fell each year, were used to set the next year's budget. Realising that the budget process served no purpose, the accountants now simply take Martin's projected cost for the forthcoming year.

Reflect on that: no time wasted in monthly budget reviews. Instead, the focus for day-to-day management is knowledge of how the system consumes money, which is also used to project future costs. Another knock-on consequence has been the disbanding of "performance management" teams whose task of monitoring KPIs, largely achievement of activity targets, is now redundant.

We will return to housing repairs when we discuss IT systems (chapter 8), for it is common in repairs systems to use standard bought-in IT packages for scheduling, something, as we will show, that actually drives the system out of control. Martin abandoned his conventional IT scheduling system and developed his own at a fraction of the cost.

Summary:

Budget management is of no value in understanding or improving operations.

Study reveals how current budget-based controls cause sub-optimisation.

Three primary controls, first developed in the studying phase, are employed to understand and control operations.

The ability to predict performance obviates the need for time-consuming and expensive conventional budget management.

The results are transformational: far better service at lower cost.

5 People-centred services

In our initial assignments with public services, we helped leaders transform individual service streams – council tax, benefits, homelessness, housing, social care, among others. Working also with police and fire and rescue teams, we began to realise that many of the people presenting to them were already known to the authorities through transactions with other services. In other words, a disproportionate volume of services was being consumed by the same relatively small group of people, whose lives for one reason or another had gone off track. From this realisation grew the idea of designing services that were what we thought of as "citizen-shaped". As this work developed, we came to label them "people-centred services".

People's lives fall off the rails in a variety of ways. The public services provided to respond to their needs are wide-ranging, potentially involving one or more of police, fire and rescue, health, mental health, care and voluntary services, attending to needs of many types. Sitting atop their inherent expertise-based organisations, and beginning in Margaret Thatcher's reign as Prime Minister, successive governments imposed command-and-control management practices in the name of "New Public Management". These had the aim of increasing efficiency and lowering costs. Instead, as illustrated in previous examples, the interventions caused massive unintended consequences through the imposition of dysfunctional means of control. *

In the face of abundant and continuing evidence of failing services and rising costs, successive governments have demonstrated the strength of their unswerving faith in command-and-control ideas by demanding that providers do more of the same, only faster and better. As Russ Ackoff taught us, like all attempts to do "the wrong thing righter", this only makes them wronger. As we have seen, conventional controls provide no indication of, or even window on,

---

* Seddon, J., (2014). *The Whitehall Effect*. Axminster: Triarchy Press.

the way the controls themselves sub-optimise performance. Instead politicians, who believe things are as tight as a drum, are beguiled by the way, over time, services become reported as "on target", whereas the time taken to get "on target" is actually a reflection of the time it took public-sector managers' ingenuity to work out how to at least appear to be on target by gaming the system. *

Take targets for carrying out assessments in care services, for example. An assessment takes place every time a patient or client is referred to a different service or department, which can be multiple times for reasons we explain shortly. In these circumstances, meeting targets for assessments simply covers up the terrible truth: the extraordinary time it actually takes for people to get through the red tape, the mind-boggling number of people involved, the forms, assessments, administration, reminders, means testing and, most insulting of all, the "friends and family test" – would you recommend this service to your friends and family? – do nothing to turn around the life of a person in need. But it is the stuff of the command-and-control regime, which blinds it to the dysfunction it causes.

When leaders study their service through the eyes of the customer or citizen, this is what they find. If your life comes apart and you approach your local authority for help, you may be seen by a dozen or more people, each of them dutifully meeting their activity targets for conducting assessments, considering your needs through their own specialist lens, being encouraged to refer you elsewhere so they can class your case as "closed", protecting their stretched budgets by imposing "thresholds" to weed out those judged insufficiently needy, and each asking questions you have already answered several times already. If after all that you do qualify for a service, it is likely to be an offering that doesn't meet your needs. Many services are commissioned, the idea being that putting the service out to the market will drive down costs. For suppliers to quote a price

---

* Seddon, J., (2008). See Chapter 8: 'Deliverology': *Systems Thinking in the Public Sector*. Axminster: Triarchy Press

in their tender, a specification is required, so the service is usually standardised. But standardised services inevitably fail to match the variety of people's needs, providing some things that don't help and others that go further than necessary, both of which having to be paid for even if they are not value work. If, having been provided with help that didn't, you take your problem back again (failure demand) you will be subjected to the same labyrinthine treatment. Any semblance of a relationship having evaporated, you will likely be treated as a new case and quite frequently offered the same service that failed to help the first time. If you have the temerity to turn it down, you risk being labelled difficult or recalcitrant.

(To return for a moment to our discussion on the nature of this change, many leaders of public services might read the paragraph above and be outraged. Our plea to them is go study.)

The backbone of the control system is the management of activity and cost, which is what the bureaucracy demands must be measured and accounted. When people come back, as they do, to get their unsolved problem fixed, it is not recognised as failure demand; it is counted as new activity to be processed though the same insensitive machine. Even while the system can show it meets its targets, its purpose of putting a life back on track is lost and undermined. While it proudly reports meeting its budget, it wastes enormous sums of public money. While commissioners can show control of commissioned services by pointing to suppliers' adherence to Key Performance Indicators, having lost sight of their purpose they have no idea of the real effectiveness of the services they pay for.

The first clue, as ever, is the volume of failure demand entering the system. But, as you will now be aware, the only way to eradicate it is to alter the system to prevent it occurring in the first place. The best case for changing the system comes from studying people-centred services – not least because of all the services described in this book, people-centred services turn out to be the easiest to study.

Paradoxically, it is the bureaucracy developed over recent years that is to thank for that, in the shape of the records it maintains of transactions between public services and the public they serve. We have helped leaders study many cases, and virtually all of them display the same features: inordinate numbers of assessments, referrals, rationing/refusal of support by threshold, and, after all that – or more accurately, because of all that – a stunning failure to meet the purpose of helping people to get themselves back on track. Study graphically shows how most services fail to meet their first and most important test – responding effectively to the variety of customer demands. When extensive maps of transactions are posted around a room and one asks the question, "At what point did we understand this person, what happened to them, what context it occurred in and what mattered to them?", the answer most often is never.

> *Paul's life fell off the rails. Over a period of 10 months, he was the subject of 179 activity records by public servants, involving 91 staff from 20 different teams. He experienced 12 assessments and 11 referrals, leading to six hospital admissions with total stays of 81 days, while staff generated seven support plans. At no point did anyone spend time with Paul to understand what mattered and what "success" might mean to him.*

Bureaucracy imposes unnecessary cost. Yet this pales into insignificance compared with the costs of providing services that are ineffective. The political narrative is driven by the unquestioned assumption that demand is rising and someone has to pay – this is the whole basis for austerity, for example. Yet the evidence suggests that demand – at least the original "my-life-has-fallen-off-the-rails" demand – is stable. It is failure demand that is growing inexorably. The truer narrative is that services are ineffective and thus waste massive amounts of public funds. But failure demand can be eliminated. Doing so increases capacity as it strips out fake demand and unnecessary cost. Effective service costs less.

Budget management is at the heart of the current dysfunction. It forces service provision to be constrained by allocating monies to specified services. Domiciliary Care, Day Services, Respite Care, Residential, Nursing, Learning Disability, Children's Mental Health, Adult Mental Health, Sheltered Housing, Physical Disability, Carer Services, Drug Therapies, Obesity Services, Smoking Cessation, Sexual Health and so on – the labels vary around the country – each has its own individual "pot" of money and accompanying budget, against which the management bureaucracy will be held to account. In effect, budget management determines the offerings that each service can and cannot provide.

Budget management is exercised through commissioning, with sometimes dysfunctional results as budgets for some services are spread over a number of commissioners. This is the case, for example, with the budgets for sexual and reproductive health.

> *A coil (long-acting reversible contraceptive device) can be fitted by a GP, but he or she must identify whether the fit is to stop bleeding or to prevent pregnancy in order to decide who to invoice for the fit. The answer is invariably that it is for both, and the commissioner who pays the most receives the bill.*

> *A person suffering from a genital dermatology problem who first presents at a sexual health clinic, unaware their condition is not sexually transmitted, may be turned away or referred on to dermatology services, despite the fact that the sexual health clinic has the expertise to manage the condition.*

In sum, what drives behaviour are rules on commissioning, not patient demand.

The problem – as by now you will probably have figured out – is that the "pots" don't fit people. They are a constraint on the delivery of services; budget management and the way it is allocated to commissioning responsibilities enshrines the fragmentation of services, ensuring that decisions about provision are budget-based (what we can spend money on) not person-based (what someone needs). Many people who are judged as having "insufficient needs" will be left for the condition to get worse, ensuring greater consumption of resources later. Others will "over-consume" resources, unnecessarily spent because they fail to help. Managing costs *causes* costs.

Meanwhile, assessment of management's performance will be based on achievement of activity and cost (numbers of citizens seen, assessed and/or closed, and provided with services, and costs compared to the budget) rather than how well the services worked for recipients. These two primary system conditions, activity management and budget management, are the control mechanisms that have the reverse effect, driving the system out of control.

To address the purported crisis in health and care services, government has adopted two general strategies: commissioning – as mentioned earlier, using the market to drive costs down – and "strategic reviews", a euphemism for cutting services back.

Commissioning services

Government guidance advises commissioners to adopt a "commissioning cycle" in which it will "identify the benefit, decide how to achieve it, commission services and monitor them". This sounds reasonable on the surface, but does it constitute a sound method? How do commissioners identify the benefit? What commissioners don't do is study demand in the way we describe it here. They often tell us their work is solidly based on demand, but on investigation it always turns out that they mean *historical provision* (for example, the number of drug-treatment programmes provided last year), assuming, wrongly, that that tells us something about demand. Commissioners have no knowledge of the effectiveness of their service, and how ineffectiveness drives failure demand.

Government insists commissioners should focus on "outcomes". Despite this, the "performance data" (KPIs) are typically the usual activity statistics. How many people have been assessed? Were assessments completed in target times? How many services were provided? Was the budget adhered to? By this sleight of hand "outcomes" come to be represented by the output of providers, not results experienced by those receiving the services.

Commissioners see their challenge as purchasing services while staying in budget. This means that price frequently becomes a determining factor in the choice of provider. In practice, the focus on price has two perverse consequences: mass-produced, standardised services that fail to meet the variety of needs, which also rules out a "thermostatic" approach (so you get 30 minutes regardless of whether 10 or 40 might have been better); and unnecessary volumes of activity (since that is how providers are paid).

Another factor reinforcing the status quo is that in a previous life many commissioners were local-authority leaders who ran the services they are now buying, in traditional command-and-control manner. Some authorities have seized on the opportunity to outsource all their services, retaining only the managers who used to run them in the role of commissioners. The results are as we might expect. Brought up, as they have been, on the principles of New Public Management, such commissioners have no new ideas to bring to the design of services or the activity and service-level measures that they judge suppliers by.

Meanwhile, the commissioner / provider split might have been designed to make any collaborative focus on effective design near impossible. Providers are obliged to comply with the performance measures commissioners specify, and use that ("we give you the performance data you ask for") as a defence against commissioners taking a closer look at real outcomes for the customer. At worst, the focus on price and meeting the budget gives both commissioners and providers a shared incentive to cast a discreet veil over what is actually happening to people who need help. Moreover, in many areas providers are large and have no competition, leaving authorities with no choice about whom to commission. This again discourages closer cooperation.

Operationally, providers under pressure of rising costs are frequently on the phone to commissioners to ask for greater provision – more time to give to tasks, and/or more tasks to be provided to individuals. Recourse to the "safeguarding team" becomes an option when the gap between what they are commissioned to provide and the needs of vulnerable individuals gets too wide. Managers in provider organisations spend 90% of their time on the bureaucracy of time sheets, expenses claims, checking attendance, tracking down social workers, progress-chasing requests for changes to provision with commissioners, and the like. Fire-fighting to meet KPIs means that stress levels are high and morale low, exacerbated by the knowledge that continuity of support is poor and outcomes for the recipients of service less than satisfactory. Indeed, complaints are frequent.

The fact is that the way services are commissioned makes it almost impossible to do the job properly. The focus on price leads to services being commissioned on a time and task basis – a specified amount of time for a specified service. But commissioning specified services means telling providers what they *won't* be paid for – things like cleaning, taking out the rubbish, shopping, lighting the fire, help with making friends, overcoming loneliness, improving the quality of life – since these are not care needs as defined in the contract. The providers' rotas and specifications drive what care staff are allowed to do, taking away autonomy, judgement and initiative, having an adverse impact on morale. In many cases care staff do do what matters, but "under the radar". Providers feel they put huge effort into providing the service but are dismayed by the feelings of failure and of not being able to truly help.

The dysfunction is evidenced by many absurdities.

A man being cared for had grown very long toenails. The care provider had to tell the commissioner (rather than cut the nails). It took three months to arrange a visit by a chiropodist. The one thing you can predict is that toenails will continue to grow, but the commissioning regime makes it impossible to plan ahead. The next time the nails need cutting, the referral process has to start again.

A quadriplegic man was discharged from hospital. He was entitled to adaptations to his home, most of which had been installed. The remaining problem was his use of the kitchen. The local authority offered to either renew the kitchen or help him move house, since it had budgets for these activities. What the man actually needed was a hydraulic lift for his chair. But for that there was no budget.

When the whole system – commissioners and providers – is studied it is clear that all parties share the conviction that demand is rising. They believe demand is greater than the ability to supply. Commissioners are blamed for not providing enough money, commissioners blame government for not providing enough money. All parties assume that the only thing worth discussing is who will have to pay.

Meanwhile providers are also often perversely incentivised to do the wrong thing. For example, a GP practice manager, when asked to take part in the National Diabetes Prevention programme aimed at reducing the prevalence of diabetes amongst their at-risk patients, refused to refer patients to the programme because the practice would receive less money for prevention than for treating a patient who had developed the condition. We have seen the same in hospitals, with patients being prioritised for treatment according to the monies their condition attracts. These are not bad people. These are bad systems.

Strategic reviews

The second means government uses to tackle the "care crisis" is "strategic review", aka cost-cutting. The (false) starting assumption here is that resources are already stretched as tight as possible. The big budget numbers comprising staff and service provision costs, the response to what's described as the "austerity agenda" is either to restrict access to services, or reduce services, or both. Thresholds for service are increased, recruitment halted, allocation panels delayed or stopped, and some services discontinued. In choosing the latter, government requires health-service leaders to create two lists, one comprising services that could in all likelihood be discontinued without causing a local outcry, the second services whose loss would be more controversial, decisions about which would be made by the government. If ministers had an inkling of how these services use money, understanding the distinction between productive and unproductive use, they would be in a position to make more constructive decisions.

> *A local authority decided to save money by closing day-centres for people with learning disabilities, replacing them with lower-cost services in the community. But the service users hadn't suddenly lost their needs; meeting them in a different way required greater provision of day-services in their homes (paid from a different budget), which turned out to be more expensive than the day-centres.*

When considering budget cuts, local-authority managers start from the view that they are more or less locked in to services already contracted, so opportunities for cuts must be sought in contracts viewed as "discretionary".

Triangle of needs

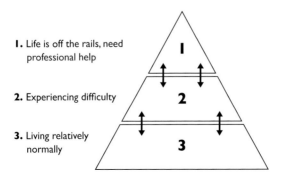

1. Life is off the rails, need professional help
2. Experiencing difficulty
3. Living relatively normally

Commissioners, particularly those who were previously managers in local authorities, like to talk about people's "triangle of needs" (see figure). Those at the bottom – the vast majority – are assumed to be capable of taking a do-it-yourself approach to care service needs. Those "experiencing difficulty" in the middle tier are acknowledged to be in need of some help but in view of budget constraints are ineligible for commissioned services, which are reserved for those at the top whose lives are in serious disarray.

In practice, what happens is that those in the middle are left to get worse.

We also conceptualise the hierarchy of needs as a triangle, but with a different interpretation of the relationship between the tiers. Living relatively normal lives, most of us at the bottom of the triangle have little need for state support, and when we do seek a service we expect it to work. In the middle, some individuals or families run into difficulties of various kinds – which current commanded-and-controlled service methods are likely to make worse, driving them into the neediest band at the apex of the triangle where they really do require help. Instead, the focus should be on helping them to get back to normal as quickly as possible, as they would want. Greater effectiveness, better outcomes, lower costs.

After commissioning and strategic reviews, as a last resort there is a third and even cruder method managers use to cut costs. This is labelled "managing demand", in essence rationing by another name: limiting services, finding excuses to turn people away and second-guessing professional decisions – reviewing GP referrals to hospital, for instance. For a fuller discussion of the folly of managing demand see chapter 20 of *The Whitehall Effect.** The bottom line: we don't need to "manage" demand, we need to understand it. Understanding demand is management treasure: a lever for improvement that is simply out of reach to command-and-

---

* Seddon, J., (2014). *The Whitehall Effect*. Axminster: Triarchy Press, 2014

control management teams: if followed through, it leads logically to what any manager, commissioner or government department would die for, a close fit of provision to need, the frugal use of resources to maximum effect.

People in difficulty want choice, involvement, relationships, consistency and continuity; in general they don't want to go into a home, which is the last (and most expensive) resort. In short, they want these services to respond to what matters to them.

Surprising as it may seem to some, this is perfectly possible – if we go beyond command and control. To design an effective service that meets these predictable, ordinary needs, we return to our three primary controls: the understanding of demand, the value work and achievement of purpose. Recall first that study of the system almost always shows that at no point are those in need asked what they are actually in need of. Because of the system conditions under which they operate, the focus of service providers is what's right for us as opposed to what's right for you. And recall that demand is the greatest lever in transactional services. So understanding demand in citizen terms is crucial to an effective design. The expertise required is, to put it simply, the competence to listen, understand and help the citizen be clear about what matters to them.

In these more effective designs, all demand – people putting their hand up for help – is met by someone going directly out to meet them. No forms, no signposting, no remote contact, no standardised assessment, and no denial of service. The focus of the meeting is to establish what has happened to the citizen, the context – what is going on in his/her life – in the family, the community, or whatever it is that's relevant to the presenting demand. Having understood the need and context, the next step is to help the citizen to establish what, for them, would be a good result. What do you need to live a good life in your terms? Or, it sometimes may be, what do you need to die a good death? The third step is to determine what the citizen can do to take responsibility in achieving that end. Then, and only then, the helper can determine what further support they need from family, from community, from the voluntary sector, or from the state, to get there. The provision of specialist expertise is only applied where it is needed and where it is proportionate to actual needs – meeting the recipient's definition of a "better" life.

In a command-and-control perspective, such a simple approach is frighteningly open-ended; where is the control? In real life, what happens is nothing short of amazing. Lives get put back on the rails, often quickly once the real need is identified. The cost of services provided falls dramatically – listening doesn't cost much – and, the greatest prize of all, as individuals and families are straightened out and stop coming to the notice of the police, education authorities or social services, overall demand begins to fall away. Does this sound too good to be true? It is the result of using effective controls; a thorough understanding of demand, a focus on doing only the value work and achievement of purpose in the care recipients' terms.

> *Julie, head of adult services in a county council, describes the change as moving from asking "What's the matter with you?" to "What matters to you?" Asking the former leads a service down the path of prescribing a set of predetermined service-driven solutions to a problem. The latter leads to a conversation about what a good life looks like to an individual citizen. That conversation may require two hours, two weeks or even two years to answer fully, but the important thing is to get a complete picture of the citizen and his or her requirements in their own context. Asking different questions is just the start; combining the answers with a system redesigned to cope with the inevitable variety of responses leads to a profoundly different set of outcomes. It delivers bespoke, personalised solutions that put back – as far as is possible – independence and resilience into people's lives. Proof of the pudding: the authority has underspent its adult services budget in successive years, and there has been a concomitant drop in demand into the service from 8000 to 3000 cases a year.*

In a municipality in the north of Sweden, care-service leaders wanted to solve the problem of continuity, a critical issue for so many people receiving care. They had already redesigned the services to be "thermostatic", adjusting to the urgency or "temperature" of the presenting conditions on the spot. That made availability less predictable – so how could continuity in the caring relationship be ensured? It appears a difficult problem, but one quickly solved by understanding how to measure and manage variation – as we described with the housing repairs case in the last chapter.

Overcoming the usual stand-off with care providers, a commissioner in Wales launched a joint initiative to study their common system. Faced with clear evidence of its ineffectiveness, the parties developed a commissioning strategy based on analysis of demand in a geographic area that gave discretion to care workers to do what mattered for individuals on a thermostatic basis. Care quality improved and costs fell. Both parties understood the importance of controlling the services by understanding demand and capacity.

Summary:

People-centred services represent a huge opportunity to go beyond command-and-control to offer a much closer fit between public-service provision and users' real needs, getting both lives and public services back on track

Budget management is the primary cause of sub-optimisation in people-centred services. It drives up ineffectiveness and thus costs.

Demand for people-centred services is stable, failure demand grows like yeast.

Three same primary controls drive up effectiveness and capacity, reduce costs and get more lives back on the rails.

Shouldn't that be the purpose of people-centred services?

6 The better philosophy

All of the examples you have read so far share the following features, features that distinguish them from command-and-control management:

The perspective taken is "outside-in" (that is, standing in the customer's shoes) rather than top-down, and work is designed according to the principles of demand, value and flow (just doing the value work) instead of being divided into functional specialisms. Decision-making is integrated with work, and conventional measures are either abandoned or relegated to "lagging" status (i.e. not used for making decisions). Management's role is to act on the system of work rather than manage people and budgets. The attitude towards customers is "what matters". There is no hiding behind notions of contractual obligations, and suppliers are treated as part of the system, collaborators rather than organisations to be squeezed or coerced. The approach to change starts with acquiring knowledge by studying operations as a system. Change being treated as emergent, there is no longer need for plans, cost-benefit analyses, deliverables and project management; instead decision-making is based on confidence in the direction of improvement, even though the precise extent cannot be calculated in advance.

Leaders manage the system with an emphasis on its purpose in customer terms, confident that financial results follow. Leaders no longer focus on managing cost, having learned how managing cost drives costs up. Instead their focus is on managing value – by which we mean designing services to ensure customers get what they need. Command-and-control thinkers assume this can only drive costs up, but the opposite is the case: it drives costs out of the system. Leaders know that demand is the great lever – and appreciate the folly of treating all demand as work to be done. Designing against demand eradicates failure demand, increasing capacity. The primary controls are derived from the purpose of the service from the customers' point of view; the consequent knowledge diminishes the need for budget management, relegating cost and revenue to the status of lagging measures.

The first thing many people say when visiting an organisation employing the Vanguard Method (not something we would encourage, by the way – see the Epilogue) is, "What did you do to the people?" They notice that levels of motivation (entirely intrinsic, all carrots, sticks and other extrinsic forms of motivation having been swept away) are extraordinarily high. They see that workers and managers have complementary roles; everyone from the front line to top leadership shares the same perspective of working on the system. This is not the result of a "culture change"; nothing was done to the people. But the positive impact on morale of being able to do a good job, and knowing it, is palpable. Sickness, absenteeism and staff turnover fall. Culture change, a lagging indicator, comes free.

The starting place – which we *would* encourage – is to look inside your own operation and study the service as a system.

The nature of this change: a leader's journey

It is a frequently cited axiom that there is no change without leadership, and when the change, as in the case for going beyond command and control, represents a fundamental shift in thinking, it will not happen unless leaders are fully aware of what that means for them and the system of which they are part. So here we aim to bring to life the leadership challenge by describing the learning journey of a typical leader - starting by helping them make what we call the invisible visible.

Andrea was in charge of a home claims business, part of an insurance division of a large UK bank. She had become curious about our work via one of her colleagues who had taken a master's degree of which the curriculum included the theory and practice of the Vanguard Method. The insights he was passing on as a result of studying demand were enough to get us through the door. When we met, we learned that she was happy that most of her measures were, and would be, "green" (especially on the Thursday morning performance review call with her boss), but costs were rising and customer-satisfaction scores were poor. We also learned that most of her time was taken up in project review meetings. There were 35 initiatives underway, representing £20m of projected "savings" and service "improvements". Given the sums invested, project milestones and deliverables were reviewed daily. So while Andrea had expressed an interest in exploring new ways of working, her focus was on delivering the current activity and keeping the status lights green. As such, the idea of finding time in her diary to study her system was unthinkable (after all, wasn't that why she employed people to manage change?).

So the immediate challenge was to coax Andrea out of her current world, where her time was entirely consumed by the demands of command-and-control management, to a different place where she could appreciate the real needs and experiences of customers. That would expose the currently invisible assumptions governing how the business was controlled, and how those controls in turn affected performance and, in particular, costs.

For instance, it stood out to the interventionist supporting Andrea that some of the current "improvement" projects were unlikely to generate much or indeed any value. Thus, large sums of money were being spent on new call-routing technology to make it easier for customers to get through to the person handling their claim (agents worked in specialised teams, depending on the nature of the claim, and calls were often misrouted). At first glance that might appear sensible. But to find out if it really was such a good idea, we would want Andrea to go back a step and question why these calls occurred in the first place (double-loop learning). How many of them were failure demands? We'd also want her to question the language used in the customer telephony options – were they in off-putting business jargon, or in terms the customer could relate to? One step further back still – why had she set up specialist teams in the first place? From a customer viewpoint, what value would call-routing technology add?

The unit was also investing in technology that tracked "commitments" to customers (e.g. that repairs would be done on the agreed date, contractor confirmation that a task was complete, or checking with the customer that a claim was progressing as expected). To Andrea in her current world, making and keeping on top of commitments to customers made sense, as did investing in enabling technology too. But in terms of value work from the customer's point of view, it would be apparent that such activities only serve to add cost. Behind all her change projects lay similar assumptions that we needed to encourage Andrea to question – did functional specialisation and activity management really constitute sensible means of controlling the work?

Rather than take on these specifics at the outset, and very likely become embroiled in a rational argument, it was important to help Andrea first see the whole, which would put her in a position to make these connections for herself. Where could she best gain an understanding of what was happening and why? How could she be exposed to a normative experience capable of unblocking her thinking about the design and management of her claims operation? For the interventionist, it was crucial to anchor the perspective in an outside-in, customer's point of view – so what better way than to have Andrea attend a claim visit with one of her senior claims handlers, strictly as an observer.

On the appointed day – a Wednesday – Andrea arrived at a distressing scene. The claim related to a fire that had happened the previous weekend. The house was severely damaged, the wife in tears, the husband highly agitated. Apparently impervious to the human distress, the claims adviser was busy searching for a surface on which to boot up his laptop and fill in the claim forms. He considered holding the meeting in the smoke-blackened living room whose French doors he had managed to force, before belatedly realising that that might not go down too well in the circumstances.

While he was fussing with his computer, Andrea discovered from the couple that since the fire they had been staying with welcoming neighbours, all of whom had been commendably supportive.

The claims handler's first questions were for personal details, whether the household had made previous claims or had any convictions. Extensive notes were then made about exactly when and how the fire started (the husband had been trying his hand at welding in the garage), what efforts were made to extinguish it, and the extent of the damage. Only now did the cause of the husband's distress become apparent – up to that point no one had confirmed that the accident and consequent repairs would be covered by their insurance. (Despite being asked not to react, Andrea, who was becoming increasingly twitchy as the bureaucratic and insensitive interview continued, was unable to suppress an audible sigh when the couple's minds were finally put at rest, nearly half an hour into the conversation).

The claims handler next recorded that a contractor had come out to board up the windows and doors to secure the house "So nobody could break in and steal possessions, but also for health and safety". The owners were not to enter the building. "But what about my things? Can I see if my pictures are OK?" the wife cried out, pointing tearfully to a bureau in the living-room, at the same time making clear that the main reason for her upset was worry over the fate of some emotionally precious photo albums. This was greeted with "I'm sorry but we cannot go into the building, it's unsafe", to which the wife pointed out his previous suggestion that they conduct the interview in the same room. Common sense eventually prevailed with an agreement that after completing the forms, she would be permitted to enter the room to retrieve her possessions.

When the claims handler reached the section in his script dealing with alternative accommodation, he announced that it would be provided in a four-star hotel five miles away. He became almost shirty when they reminded him that that they already had suitable accommodation (he had missed that part of the conversation fussing with his laptop), and even more agitated when they asked to have some of the cash earmarked for the hotel paid in compensation to their neighbours instead. There was nothing in his script or on the form to tell him how to handle such a request – and the visit had now taken 50 minutes, five more than the allocated 45. (He eventually got round the breach by recording that "other staff" had been present on the visit, which allowed the excess five minutes to be counted as training time.)

In the car on the return journey, Andrea expressed her horror at the behaviour she had just seen. She had moved from curious to shocked. Most sobering was the realisation that she was ultimately responsible for what she had witnessed, which was a normal human being acting on a pervasive de-facto purpose of "Follow the process, meet the target", rather than "Help the customer get back to normal life". The standardised form, its menu options and allocated 45-minute completion time, were the current means of control. She had started the day believing her teams were being genuinely helpful (weren't they all showing "green" on the status traffic lights?), but now serious doubt had crept in. Nothing she had seen gave any indication that her system was concerned with what mattered to the customer. Indeed, it hadn't escaped her notice that in the simple example of accommodation, doing what mattered to the customer by letting them stay with friends would not only make them happy but also save her company a fortune in hotel costs.

Arriving back at the office, she was "hooked". She demanded to listen to the phone call from the customer logging the claim. What she heard fitted the same pattern as in the live interview. There was no listening. The agent worked to a script, recording the same bureaucratic information – in short, following the process. Her process. Understandably, Andrea wondered if this case might have been a "stinker" – surely others couldn't be as bad? So she moved some of her project review meetings and accompanied staff on further claims visits. Her managers began to wonder what the boss was up to; not in the office, out with customers and coming back looking somewhat energised and talking about totally different things.

Her study began the process of re-thinking her beliefs. Like all command-and-control systems, Andrea's organisation was built on the assumptions that work should be functionally specialised and strongly process-driven. But the consequence – now visible to Andrea – was that frontline found themselves working in a system that discouraged them from listening. As she followed claims cases through her system, she saw people focused on "tasks", spending much of their time entering data on computer systems, handing work on, and checking and progress-chasing. Every customer call generated a series of activities and tasks sent on to others in the claims organisation and supplier networks. What mattered to managers was completing these activities in standard times and to agreed service levels while the consequences for customers went unobserved and ignored. How much of that activity was non-value work and handling failure demand was unknown, since the current perspective made it invisible. It was hardly surprising that depersonalised customers had begun to complain.

Beginning to comprehend how these activities and measures were driving costs, Andrea could also see that her current project work would do little to change things for the better. At best they might lead to improvement in some minor aspects of the work, but many would be focused on doing the wrong thing righter (thus making them wronger) as they did nothing to create value for customers. At worst, they would cement problems in. No longer could she be satisfied that her performance was green, since the measure she was using as controls were disguising the real story. They were "watermelon measures" – while they were green on the outside, the inside was bright red.

Initially daunted, Andrea was also excited by the thought of transforming her activity-led operation to one that was genuinely focused on the true purpose of its response to a claim – helping customers through their troubles to resume their normal life. To do that required her to change her measures and review her projects. She saw that initiatives designed to improve customer focus through interpersonal skills training should be replaced by a system redesign that would encourage colleagues to really listen to what customers said mattered to them; the end-to-end claims flow needed to be rethought to focus on what created value for customers. Her enthusiasm and can-do attitude led her to want nothing more than to get out among her managers to tell them what she'd learned and what she wanted them to do about it. This presented the second challenge for the interventionist: how to help Andrea lead change in a way that engaged others in a learning process rather than simply following instructions. In her excitement, she had forgotten how she had experienced the learning process herself. So when we asked her to reflect on how she would have reacted if told about the things she'd seen before she'd experienced them for herself, she realised others would, like her, simply reject or rationalise them away with, "Of course, but these are being dealt with in our plans". She decided to send her senior managers out to study, with the aim of making the invisible visible for themselves.

After a few weeks and with her operational leaders all now aligned on perspective and purpose, the scope of the challenge widened. While the priority was to establish a redesign, Andrea could see there were many other issues – system conditions – that would have to be mitigated and, ultimately, removed for the redesign to be optimal and sustainable. Key to this was establishing the new measures. This represented a logistical challenge, since the operation had not historically had the means to measure things like end-to-end times to settle a claim or the achievement of purpose from a customer's perspective. There was also the issue of reconfiguring the change programme and how to spread the new learning across the wider management community. She and her team could not do this on their own, so a "map" of key leaders (as system influencers) was drawn up. At the top of the list was the supplier management leader. In the current design the value work of assessing and fixing the claim had been outsourced. Going forward, suppliers would need to be treated as a full part of the new system and enabled to work within it in the new way.

The redesign itself was initially treated as a test. Rather than try to change the entire customer operation at one swoop, the team focused on a single geographical area where Andrea's operation and suppliers could combine pragmatically to work through claims end-to-end. The emphasis was on deploying the new principles and paying attention to the three key controls: knowledge of demand, a focus on the value work and achievement of purpose in customer terms. As the test progressed, Andrea spent more and more of her time with suppliers, judging which showed the right attitude to the methods and developing new measures to replace the existing service-level agreements. In many cases this involved unpicking and altering contractual arrangements. Back in the operation, frontline staff were coached and supported in making informed choices, enabling conversations with customers that made sense to customers but also had an effect on the bottom line. As such, the purpose of the test was to not only to prove customer benefit, but also to establish the economics of the new operation.

Results began to show through almost immediately. Within months, it was clear that failure demand was drying up and claims were being settled in a fraction of the previous time and with only half the number of transactions with customers. Customer satisfaction and staff morale within the redesign team soared. Remarkably, indemnity costs (the sums paid out to settle claims) - although not on Andrea's operational budget - also fell, with significant implications for reserve levels needed to cover future losses. As news of the unit's results spread, Andrea began to receive visitors. Consistent with what the team had learned, visiting executives were guided through a normative experience; starting with the old business as usual, then what was learned through study, next the principles governing the redesign and, finally, the redesign in action.

As the empirical data and insights from the work accumulated, so did the knowledge and understanding of Andrea and her leadership team in terms of their new roles. The process of unlearning and learning beyond command and control not only enabled them to make informed decisions as to what to do, but also how to do it. In the course of the journey, they had left command and control behind and become systems leaders. Importantly, embedding new leadership principles and practices gave them the insight and confidence to scale up the redesign, working to the principle of "rolling in" (first helping people change their ways of thinking) as well as to engage with other, wider influencers across the support functions of finance, risk, HR and IT. All, ultimately, needed to understand and change the way they worked to align with, and sustain, the principles in the redesign, thus moving beyond command and control. We have plenty more to say about tackling these in Part 2.

Part 2:

Changing thinking about the management factory

7 The growth of management controls

In 1988 Peter Drucker wrote:

> *"The typical large business 20 years hence will have fewer than half the levels of management of its counterpart today, and no more than a third the managers"* *

Peter Drucker should have been right. But he reckoned without the logic of command and control – thanks to which the opposite has happened. While many large service organisations have striven to flatten the hierarchy, this has not prevented the number of those employed in jobs sitting above the customer-facing front line from mushrooming. Almost all these jobs are concerned with control. HR, finance, audit, compliance, IT, performance management: all of these are control functions, on top of and as well as the management mechanisms we have discussed already. Going beyond command and control requires a re-think of what these functions are for and, more critically, a change in perspective in which hierarchical control gives way to enabling effective control; support rather than control.

In the early 1960s, the Tavistock Institute's Eric Trist made an important (and still neglected) discovery. Working with the then National Coal Board, he found that the much anticipated productivity gains from large-scale pit mechanisation were disappointing or even negative – except in one seam where workers had been allowed to develop their own cooperative way of working, with dramatically better results. From this emerged the idea of "socio-technical systems", which recognised that humans and machines, being interdependent, neither could be optimised at the expense of the other. However, despite the profound improvements

---

* https://hbr.org/1988/01/the-coming-of-the-new-organization

in morale, attendance and productivity, Trist was dismayed when the board rejected his proposal to extend the new way of thinking more generally. The blunt reality was that, in an era of hostile management-union relations, managers simply could not accept the idea of the workers having control. In effect, they regarded control as more important than productivity. (To be fair, even the unions were opposed to workers being implicated in management).

In the years since then, countless programmes of empowerment, engagement, culture change and the like have attempted to involve workers in decision-making – and failed, since there was no diminution of the underlying management obsession with control. Given that we are all supposed to be knowledge workers now, one might hope that today's leaders would take a more constructive view of the potential for improving productivity through changing their theories of control, putting it in the hands of workers where the work is done.

Understanding what the hierarchical management functions do and how they impact on the system is not the jumping-off point for leaving command and control behind. That should always begin with operations. But the understanding is essential if leaders are to maintain the redesigned system.

We have come to think of the typical organisation's superstructure of control as the "management factory". We coined this perhaps somewhat pejorative term in the 1990s when, observing a large blue-chip IT organisation, we were struck by the evident divide between operations and management, as though there were two systems, not one. Getting on in the management factory seemed to be dependent on having and being able to present good ideas – at least perceived as good by current norms – usually with copious PowerPoint presentations. Occupants of the management factory would make occasional forays into operations to intervene – make changes – without ever staying around long enough to see if the interventions had even been delivered, let alone whether they were effective or not.

In the management factory, initiatives are usually evaluated for being on plan rather than actually working. Often there is so much change, or interference, going on that it is difficult to attribute outcomes to any one initiative – added complications being that failures are rarely talked about and protagonists move on before results are apparent. In any case, even substantial failure – such as channels stuffed with failure demand – is often invisible to leaders because of the blind spots in their control systems, as we have discussed and will shortly return to with digital initiatives.

The writer and consultant Gary Hamel estimates that in US organisations as much as 80% of the workforce is employed in the management factory. In the UK we find much the same. For Hamel, this growth slows decision-making, focuses on internal organisational issues, creates roadblocks to innovation, discourages risk-taking and concentrates energy on protecting or growing "turf". Managers themselves report that much of their time is devoted to bureaucratic chores, in particular meetings, and getting innovations off the ground is difficult. Less obviously but worse, hierarchy, argues Hamel, increases the risk of calamitous major decisions – as decisions get bigger, the ranks of those able to challenge them get smaller, and the people at the top who make the decisions are least likely to be challenged.

There are two more insidious systemic reasons for concern. Decisions about change or improvement, whether large- or small-scale, are grounded firmly in the current command-and-control philosophy with its inherent bias towards improving the wrong things, such as transaction costs and service levels. Second, many of the management-factory functions actively propagate system conditions that sub-optimise performance. From the point of view of overall performance, using "best practice" in HR, audit, finance and IT, for example, is neither best nor even good.

How do leaders make decisions about improvement?

When leaders set out on improvement initiatives, they naturally assume their decisions are rational and soundly based. In fact, of course, they are based on the philosophy of command and control and grounded in its associated measures. As you will be aware from the preceding chapters, these measures not only do not represent knowledge of true performance, they push it in the wrong direction.

One consequence of the growth of the management factory is the increasing remoteness of top leaders from operations. This is rationalised by the argument that it helps to make decisions more objective. Good governance, it is argued, requires a hierarchical structure. Changes, therefore, are presented to the upper echelons of the hierarchy, decided on at this highest level, handed down for implementation and reviewed for compliance.

Change proposals come from a host of possible functions – business development, IT analysis, organisation development, improvement – on the basis of performance information gathered from operations on costs, variance from budget, activity statistics, sales, productivity, customer satisfaction, service-levels and the like, supplemented by questionnaires or interviews with operations managers. The competing change programmes are presented in a flurry of papers and PowerPoint "decks" to the leader who will choose between them. Unfortunately, since the plans are invariably formulated with no real grounding in the "what and why" of performance, the consequences of all that effort bear no relation to the outcomes confidently predicted.

We can – and should – radically cut back the effort that goes into making plans; change without knowledge is perilous. Two things are necessary:

- Ensuring that leaders are completely knowledgeable about operations as a requirement for determining what to change
- Making the decisions at the lowest hierarchical level

When these conditions are met, the need for an unwieldy bureaucratic planning and decision-making crowd dissolves.

Knowledge: the prerequisite for effective change

We have described how to "get knowledge", and emphasised that it is the leaders' responsibility to do so. Leaders must treat the acquisition of knowledge about the "what and why" of performance as a system as their responsibility and live by the rule that no change will occur without that knowledge and the consequential ability to predict in what direction measures will improve. Armies of proposers, planners, cost-benefit calculators and project managers are simply not needed. Other functions of the management factory should be enjoined to the study work as a preliminary step in re-focussing and re-sizing their activities. Later chapters describe how this happens with two of the most critical – IT and HR – but here we mention the importance of involving three other control functions: audit, risk and regulation. The extent to which their involvement is critical varies according to the power they wield in the organisation. To take each in turn:

Audit

Audit practice varies from an inspection to a formative ethos, the latter setting out to provide help and advice on improvement. Some audit functions focus mainly on financial probity; others work to a wider brief. Regardless, if the audit function is one that inculcates any sense of concern for leaders its representatives ought to be involved in the study work, for the simple reason that the operational controls will inevitably change and the auditor should experience the same normative shift as their line-manager colleagues, lest "rational" blocks occur that will only serve to slow things down.

Risk

A relatively new function, focused on asking "what could go wrong?", and making contingent plans to "manage" those possibilities. The study phase addresses two different and more useful questions: "what does go wrong?" and "how predictable are these failures?" As we have shown, plenty goes "wrong" in command-and-control systems. All of the predictable failures are under the control of leaders; this stark realisation is revealed through studying; knowledge becomes the antidote to "risk".

Regulation

Regulation varies enormously between sectors. Where regulators limit their edicts to matters of purpose (for example "know your customer" in financial services), as they should, and refrain from prescribing the methods or measures to be employed, it is generally plain sailing to ensure the emergent design fits well with the regulator's purpose. However, it is frequently the case that internal regulatory functions add their own views as to how the stated purpose should be achieved, and these are likely to be grounded in the command-and-control philosophy. In that case, the same principle applies: involve these players in the study phase in order that they re-think the means for complying with the regulator's purpose. We have found that regulators, by and large, are open to better means of control, frequently citing novel systems designs as exemplary.

From control to support

From a base of knowledge rather than opinion and command-and-control ideas about control, these central functions shift from a focus of control to one of support. If, as it should be, the focus of service operations is to create value for customers, then the focus of the central functions should be to create value for the front line, the place where organisations make or use money. In today's world, probably the most important function to re-think is IT, which needs to re-think not only its purpose as support rather than control (for it has become the de facto means through which command and control is exercised in organisations) but also its entire modus operandi. For that reason, IT is the subject of the next four chapters. We then move on to HR.

8 Putting Information Technology in its place

IT has come to dominate the way organisations work. Without IT
we would never have had today's mass-produced, industrialised
services, structured around service centres and front-, back- and
middle-offices, whose life-blood is workflow systems and whose
controls, hard-wired in IT, are reporting activity at a micro level.
(By now you might be able to guess where "middle offices" came
from. That's right: another symptom of command-and-control
dysfunction, they were invented by Big Consultancies to progress-
chase, re-allocate and otherwise do anything to get productivity
moving as their front and back offices progressively clogged up
with failure demand. You couldn't make it up.)

One thing is clear: it is difficult to think of running our organisations
without IT. But it is also clear that, as currently employed, IT, as the
infrastructure backbone for industrialised services, is a big part of
the problem.

Even in its own terms, it is not sufficiently known that behind its
ubiquitous presence lies a breaker's yard of scrapped and failed
schemes. The IT industry prefers not to talk about it, but 30% of
large-scale IT projects fail completely and a further 60% partially,
in that they require more time, resource and effort and/or still do not
meet requirements. *

This isn't because IT is inherently useless or wrong, but because
it is too often used to do things that are non-essential or shouldn't
be done at all. The industry has little incentive to concern itself
with non-technological reasons for failure and plenty to move
on as quickly as possible to the next hot idea, thus reinforcing
the ever-increasing technological fetishisation. ERM, CRM, the
Cloud, work-flow, scheduling, dashboards, digitalisation, artificial

---

* Gauld, R. and Goldfinch, S., (2006). *Dangerous Enthusiasms.
E-government, Computer Failure and Information System Development.*
New Zealand: Otago University Press

intelligence, Big Data, robotics – each is offered as superseding the last and a "must-have" benefit rather than the mere additional feature it often is. In the abstract, the promises seem compelling, creating bandwagons that managers fear not to join. And as any new technical feature is adopted it dictates and underpins the logic employed in the management factory.

As services have been industrialised, as for manufacturing, the IT industry has developed specialised packages as "solutions" to its needs. The logics, inevitably, are built on command and control. As such, they comfortably fit the mind-set of a command-and-control thinker and pass quickly into common use. Sub-optimisation is institutionalised.

First, we have to declare our prejudice: IT should be the *last* thing you think about in any change, not the first, as it is at present. When IT is developed in this way, it costs vastly less and you get vastly more.

To illustrate the better way to employ information technology, we return to housing repairs. From chapter 4, you will recall that standard IT-based scheduling systems are the norm in break-fix systems. IT systems for the housing sector cost around a quarter to half a million pounds to buy and then many thousands of pounds in annual licence fees. Big companies, persuading themselves that they are unique and therefore in need of bespoke systems, can invest hundreds of millions for essentially the same kinds of "solutions".

These are sold with attractive promises, at least attractive to command-and-control thinkers: they promise to maximise the productivity of repair personnel (i.e. sweat the resource); give visibility of achievement of targets; control work activity; and, when things go wrong, modify the schedule according to your priorities. This is referred to as "dynamic scheduling", which is ironic, for the fact of the matter is that the features of the IT systems themselves create disorder and lack of control – so fire-fighting in the shape of "dynamic scheduling" becomes the norm.

These systems institutionalise the basic design steps you read about in chapter 4, making it possible to take bookings, set target dates, schedule repairs, allocate work to tradespeople – usually via a personal digital assistant (PDA) – monitor their activity and close jobs. At a more detailed level, they often provide scripts with easy-to-follow menus (embedding intelligence in the machine allows use of lower-skilled, and paid, workers to input bookings). Clicking on the type of job (e.g. bathroom, leaking tap and so on) allows the user to drill down to specific tasks for the repair, at which point the scheduling software offers the next slot when a tradesman will be available. The job as specified in the service centre will have an associated standard time which is the basis for scheduling the tradesperson and monitoring performance.

The system generates reports showing the jobs arrived at within target times, jobs with arrivals beyond target times, jobs completed according to standard times and those taking longer, all of which can be expressed in terms of RAG status. The system allows managers to choose how many jobs the tradespeople can see at one time. All of this is grist to the mill of the command-and-control manager.

But, recall what is revealed when you study these services. If the front end is "unclean" (someone who doesn't know about plumbing talking to someone else who doesn't know about plumbing, who generates a specification for someone who does), so inevitably, will be the information passed to the tradespeople. So the first thing that happens is that the IT system fills up with unclean work.

Tradespeople don't want to be punished for failing to meet targets, particularly when it's not their fault – so they use the IT system to "cancel" jobs that for whatever reason can't be completed on the scheduled visit (wrong materials, insufficient time allocated, and so on). Since tradespeople are not allowed to book jobs themselves, tenants have to call in to do so. Managers too will use the system to close a job that threatens to exceed target times and then open a "new" one to restart the clock.

The system drives both tradespeople and managers to focus on meeting target times. Alerts of jobs approaching the cut-off time spur visits by managers and other non-tradespeople just to see what the job is, as for the system this counts as meeting the target.

Such systems are prone to all the problems we saw in chapter 4. While 50% or more of the demand into the service centre is likely to be failure demand, this will not show up on the system, which can only tell managers about demand volumes, not the type. Because the work passed to tradespeople isn't "clean" (right diagnosis, right expertise, right materials, right time allocated), repair productivity is dire, with tradesmen solving problems on first visit less than 40% of the time. Managers can't see this either, as tradespeople and supervisors apply their ingenuity and the methods described above to massage their "first-time fix" numbers to keep them in the safety zone. In reality, jobs are not completed as much as 70% of the time, for reasons that by now you will be able to predict: the job, the materials or the time allocated is wrongly specified, or any combination of all three. But the system of course won't tell you that.

Managers can use the software to allocate tradesmen their daily job quota – around eight a day being considered "best practice" – via PDA. Each job is either a "morning" or an "afternoon" appointment, meaning that the tenant has to stay in for half a day or quite often more. Tenants have no choice of appointments, since the system is based on maximising resource activity. The times allocated for repairs are standardised, taking no account of variation in the work or the materials held by the tradesperson.

Quite a lot of tradespeople's ingenuity is used to get round these rigidities. For instance, they will often find a way to switch the job order to maximise bonus points, which may push the visit into a different half day. Or when confronted with a job that is not the one specified by the system, they will simulate a fix so they can close the job without alerting managers changing the job code. So the world reflected by the system increasingly diverges from the real one.

Tradespeople will often not complete all of their allocated jobs. When jobs take longer than scheduled, the system will re-allocate the work, causing managers to lose sight of who is doing what and lose control of the work. Managing reactively rather than having active control of the work, managers end up having only the sketchiest idea of what is going on in their system, and no notion at all of how the way in which they manage robs them of capacity.

Like any attempt to exert standardised control over a dynamic reality, such systems dismally fail to reach their promised productivity levels – more than 30% of tradespeople's time and effort are unproductive.

When leaders study their system, they witness all the above at first hand. They learn that they have been taken in by the IT vendor's claims. They can see that what they thought were their "controls" were in fact the opposite, and that when the RAG signals said "green" they really meant "red". But at least now they know.

What do we need from IT?

Let's step back a minute. What do we really need from IT?

This is a question that should only be addressed *after* a service has been studied and redesigned. The redesign will have established the controls that are needed to deliver an effective service. In a repairs design, we need to have a record of:

- the customer contact
- the nature of the problem (only identifiable when the tradesperson is in front of it)
- the time it will take to fix it (ditto) – which tells us when the tradesperson will be available again
- the materials used (best done on completion)

With accurate information on job type, time and materials used, we can plot the predictability of demand and from that the capacity to meet it and the necessary availability of resources. Building an IT system with these features provides complete and live visibility of all work scheduled or completed, such that leaders can allocate the correct resources on an hourly or daily basis. In other words, it gives them complete control of the work.

Start without IT

The first design has to be manual. Simple physical means, like pin-boards, T-cards and spreadsheets, record the job and what matters to the customer. Incoming work, scheduled work and work in progress are visible at a glance. Reasons for failure to complete or complete on time can be instantly spotted. Comparing current workloads with planned capacity makes capacity issues visible before they arise. The key operational measures are: type and frequency of demand, first-time resolution, end-to-end time or on-time as required. The lagging measures – which are not used for managing but which clearly show the direction of travel – are cost over time and customer satisfaction.

In this phase, if the service being redesigned uses an IT system (as is almost always the case), the IT has to be treated as a temporary constraint or where appropriate turned off.

It is only when the new design is up and running and stable, working with manual records and visible controls, that software developers can begin writing code. Even then they don't start with a specification; they start instead from first-hand knowledge of the system of work, and the organisation's purpose, methods and controls. Their focus is: now that we have a better design that is stable, how can we use IT to make the system even better, simpler, and easier to work with?

A large number of clients have taken this route, challenging their IT department to develop an IT system that is a real solution to their needs. The benefits include ownership of the code, independence from proprietary vendors charging annual fees, avoidance of the obligation to accept unnecessary upgrades to vanilla IT systems, and freedom to modify their own systems as necessary. The cost of such systems – less than £30,000 in some repairs outfits, giving them eye-watering savings and a far more effective IT system to boot.

The consequence of de-fetishising IT by putting it last is a much greater bang from much less buck; and all the code written is used – a remarkable occurrence in the IT industry.

We should also mention an IT system developed to enable redesigned repair and installation services to control material flow.* The principle is to purchase materials at the rate of use – a counterintuitive notion to a conventional manager who has been conditioned to purchase on the basis of price. The IT system uses historic data to predict material requirements, allowing purchasers control over how many days stock they want to hold. It is both simple and highly effective.

Buying for lower prices usually means buying in bulk, all too often resulting in warehouses full of materials that gather dust (or are robbed for parts). When organisations switch to buying at the rate of use, their warehouses empty out. More important, they are better at having the right materials when required (hence the increase in capacity). The same logic applies to van stocks (the items tradespeople or installers carry with them). Working with knowledge of demand, van stocks can as a rule be reduced by two-thirds while availability of the right materials is greatly improved.

We'll come back to "IT last", with further examples, when we address digital services in chapter 11. For now, we can sum up the route to effective IT systems in the following three steps: study; redesign; and only then "pull" IT. We should perhaps note in conclusion that over the last 10 years we have built a strong following among software developers, as a result of which we

* www.stockrightnow.com

have met with leaders of some of the largest software development organisations. At first they express enthusiasm for our approach, but when they learn what "IT last" means in practice, their interest quickly subsides. For them it means reduced activity – and reduced activity spells lower revenues.

9 The day we met Agile

We had recently completed an assignment helping a leader to improve mortgage lending operations at a bank. She was an impressive performer; after only a short period of studying her system she insisted the work move on to a redesign without delay. As it is the leader's pace that dictates, we helped her understand the elements that were necessary for the redesign, in parallel with starting up a proof of concept – the first step in an emergent redesign. In straitened times and within a matter of weeks, the work paid off in the shape of a massive increase in capacity and much improved customer service. As the system was scaled, sales grew with no additional resources.

The executive then moved on to another bank. Quite soon after, a group of people arrived with a mandate to "digitise" the bank (if she had stayed, it is unlikely they would have been allowed to proceed as they did). Their first initiative aimed to reduce costs by substituting databases for surveyors. Mortgage lending requires a valuation of the property. The bright idea was that the cost of human valuation could be cut by using databases of house sale prices to calculate average local property values. In no time at all there were problems. Properties are not all equivalent. Using an average inevitably causes two errors: over- and undervaluation. Overvaluation puts the lender at risk; undervaluation leads to loss of potential customers who go elsewhere for their mortgage. The idea was speedily abandoned. The digitisers were delighted with the venture, however – for them it was a great example of "fail fast" (a mantra out of the "Agile" playbook). On the other hand, we would ask: why did the initiative fail? And, moreover, why fail at all? How much did this failure cost? What are the knowable and unknowable costs?

At about the same time, we heard from a colleague of a similar occurrence in another bank. A different group, again on a mission to "digitise", had set up camp in its mortgage operation, where they busily designed and implemented a "mortgage tracker", an online tool for customers to track their application through the mortgage process. For us this was like a bad joke. By definition, tracking is most likely to be progress-chasing and therefore constitutes failure demand. In a mortgage business run on conventional command-and-control lines, it's immediately obvious to a systems thinker how the process leaves customers in the dark. With end-to-end times painfully long, and managers blissfully unaware of the fact, how could it be otherwise?

Once again – what was the point of this tracker? In our book, the first step would have been to take apart and redesign a better mortgage service. That would have resulted in shorter end-to-end times, in itself reducing uncertainty. Add a routine notification when there is a pause in the process, and customers will always know where they stand. At which point, of course, there is no longer any need for a tracker. So how much did this pointless exercise cost?

Who are these people?

At first, all we knew was that there was this group of internal and external consultants, entirely separate from operations, running programmes to digitise the banks. Then we discovered they were "Agilists" – our collective noun for people with a array of purported disciplines and titles (coach, designer, coder, scrum master, product owner – more on this later), who share a near religious belief in an approach to – well, first software development, then project management, and now almost everything – that goes under the general name of "Agile". As always when we come across something new, we ask, "Who invented this?" and, "What problem were they trying to solve?" To remove any doubt, we soon came to regard this phenomenon as possibly the most dysfunctional management fad we have ever come across.

We have written a lot about management fads*. One general observation is that they are grounded in command-and-control

---

* For critiques of many fads go to: https://vanguard-method.net/what-can-we-learn-from-programmes-of-change/

thinking: hence their appeal, and also their fatal flaw. With each, we studied what it did in practice and compared that with what could have been achieved (or avoided) if getting knowledge had been the starting point. We did the same thing with Agile. Compared with other fads, Agile purports to be the antidote to command-and-control thinking. But what it creates in its place is the opposite of reassuring.

Agile: the manifesto

Agile began life as a breath of fresh air in the IT community. It took the form of a 2001 manifesto composed by 17 software developers to channel their frustration at the all-too-frequent failure of large-scale IT systems. They argued a need to move away from conventional "waterfall" methods – sequentially writing specifications, buying hardware, writing software, testing, training people and implementing the resulting system as a big bang, all of which can take years only to end in whole or partial failure. The authors thought they knew how to do it better. Everyone likes to do a good job; software developers are as upset by failure as their customers and users. Their ambition is laudable. Getting large-scale IT projects to work, on time, matters.

The key idea in the Agile manifesto was to do this by "co-developing" applications with the people who actually use them, for example, to serve customers. No massive documentation needed before starting and no plan. Just act, respond to what is learned, pay attention to what changes, and develop solutions incrementally through rapid iterations. Sounds good, doesn't it?

A summary of the manifesto's principles: *

> *The highest priority is to satisfy the customer through early and continuous delivery of valuable software; welcoming changing requirements; delivering working software*

---

*For a full statement go to: http://agilemanifesto.org/

frequently with a preference for short timescales; business people and developers must work together; build projects around motivated individuals, giving them the environment they need; face-to-face conversation is the most efficient and effective method of conveying information; working software is the primary measure of progress; simplicity is essential; the best architectures, requirements, and designs emerge from self-organising teams; teams should reflect on how to become more effective.

The manifesto authors placed value on *individuals and interactions over processes and tools, working software over comprehensive documentation, customer collaboration over contract negotiation. and responding to change over following a plan.* All good – provided what gets developed is the right thing to make.

Again, no one would argue with the ambition:

By working more closely with the work and building solutions in iterations, IT development is live, changes can be implemented more quickly, iterations in delivery avoid the perils of batching and queuing, and Agile has learning as a key routine activity, improving what is delivered and improving future deliveries. It promises speed in delivering customer-centric design while meeting business needs.

The short timescales were labelled "sprints"; "iterations" meant taking small steps, working to create "minimum viable products", while learning through reviewing what's been done – "retrospectives". New words, new rituals; attractive, plausible.

Agile's leap from being a methodology for software development to a methodology for all ("enterprise-wide") project management was precipitated by an article in *Harvard Business Review* entitled "Embracing Agile".* The authors argued that Agile had been so successful in software development that it should now become the go-to means for organisation-wide transformation.

---

* Rigby, D., Sutherland, J., & Takeuchi, H., (May 2016) USA: HBR

Yet while it is certainly true that Agile has been widely adopted by software developers, its track record in large-scale IT development is not much better than that of waterfall. Indeed, it has been criticised even by Agile protagonists, who lament its failure to live up to the promise (see later).

Agile's track record

Large-scale failure

The UK government's IT programme for Universal Credit, announced as "digital by default" by ministers who boasted of its development using Agile methodologies, is just one notorious example of Agile's limitations – a giant "fast fail", in fact. UC was launched in 2010, the original plan calling for delivery in seven years at a cost of £2bn. The end date, which has been repeatedly moved (or "reset"), is now 2023, with the latest minister in charge warning that even this may have to be pushed back. The last available "life-cost projection" for the scheme, dating from 2015 when the project was expected to be completed by 2020, was £15.84bn. The costs do not take account of a series of additional contracts let to public- and voluntary-sector providers to mop up the failure demand created by the new system. We know that as of June 2018 running costs were £699 per UC claim – four times as much as the government had anticipated on completion. The minister – who has clearly drunk the Agile Kool-aid – valiantly claims that all will be well because the project is employing "test and learn".

Within-process waste

In large-scale transformations employing Agile, amounts of code developed (and paid for) that never gets used is anything between 50% to 80%. When you see how decisions are made about what to do (see later) this is no surprise.

Developers

Agile working hasn't prevented deep frustration among software developers who find their work stuck in a backlog or not valued by the "product owner", or, worse, the customer. They complain that product owners don't do enough to ensure alignment between strategy and tasks. In fact, they complain about a lot of things; software developers want to do good work. It is easy to find angry criticism of Agile's fitness for purpose by practitioners on the internet*.

The HBR authors made no mention of these issues; indeed, they said nothing about any failures or weaknesses (although they did admit that Agile wasn't suitable for all environments and functions, and two of their six crucial principles were "learn how Agile really works" and "understand where and when it works" – a sure warning sign of the need to beware of and puncture inflated claims). Unfortunately, unaware of or brushing aside the truth about Agile's less than stellar track record, even in software, people have queued up to swallow the extravagant claims, setting in motion a bandwagon that has swept up everything in its path. Agile has now morphed into a kind of managerial "theory of everything", its faithful currently invoking it to come to their aid in their quest for salvation through "going digital" and "digital by default".

Don't get us wrong: the Agile manifesto was a bold and worthy initiative. People were intrigued, and naturally wanted to know more. But at that point the emphasis switched from the movement to the marketable, and the spirit of the manifesto disappeared into training, consultancy, books and conferences. A market was created, which meant to find out what it all entails, in concrete terms, you have to pay.

---

* Herewith two examples of more considered critiques: www.linkedin. com/pulse/rethinking-transformation-tobias-mayer and https://queue. acm.org/detail.cfm?id=1281893

Herewith our quick guide to just some of the Agile-speak:

Agile: to make or do things through a series of iterations (make and learn)

Sprint: making something in a time-bound period (usually two weeks)

Squad / tribe: a small team / large team

Scrum: a set of rules for how a team works together

Scrum Master: The person who leads the scrum team

Stand Ups: Team meetings to review their work

Product Owner: The person who decides what a team will do; he/she represents the business and is the expert on what customers want; he/she controls the backlog and determines priorities

Human-Centred Design: Putting the customer and service agent at the forefront of what to make

Design Thinking and Ideation: dream things up

Lean Startup: when starting up a new thing, design and test as quickly as is feasible

Kanban: limit inventory and work in progress

DevOps: have the software developers and computer operations people work together

Fail Fast: You will! Agilists argue you can learn from failure. But as the pioneering systems thinker Russ Ackoff taught us, you may not learn anything from failure if what you did was the wrong thing.

We'll say more about some of these terms and introduce a few more as we go along. But let's return to Agile and digital services.

Digital services

The pitch from the Big Consultancies for going digital is generically the same as for any other IT advance: basically, since your competitors are all doing it, can you afford the risk of being left behind? "Remember Blockbuster!" they say, adding that if your industry hasn't been disrupted yet, it soon will be; and of course your customers will take for granted that there will be an app for their iPhone.

What's more – "digital services represent lower transaction costs", they will murmur, knowing that this is grist to the command-and-control thinker's mill. Agile, of course, will be the means of unlocking all these benefits.

Big Consultancies make big promises. *"We estimate that digital transformation will put upward of 30 percent of the revenues of a typical... bank in play... We also estimate that banks can remove 20 to 25 percent of their cost base by leveraging this digital shift to transform how they process and service... It's fair to say that getting digital banking right is a do-or-die challenge,"* said McKinsey, true to form, in 2014*.

Where, you might ask, is the evidence? Certainly not in the two examples we gave at the start of this chapter. We doubt that it exists. What we've seen with other examples (particularly shared services) is that Big Consultancies sometimes use "planned" improvement (conjecture in business cases) as evidence of delivered improvement. The cost-savings claimed will be based on projected volumes of transactions moving from face-to-face and telephone transactions to digital; the revenue projections will likewise be guesses. Service businesses employing the Vanguard Method have achieved comparable and better results than these – real ones, not assumptions or estimates – without "going digital" at all.

---

* The rise of the digital bank, McKinsey, July 2014, originally published in the FT, October 25, 2013.

To return to the pitch:

> *"The principles behind organisational agility are well-known by now. Agile groups can thrive in an unpredictable, rapidly changing environment. They are both stable and dynamic. They focus on customers, fluidly adapt to environmental changes, and are open, inclusive, and nonhierarchical; they evolve continually and embrace uncertainty and ambiguity."**

Of course, digital channels *are* cheaper (i.e., have lower transaction costs) – and who could be against organisational agility? But those things only matter if the new channels work, by which we mean work for customers. The problem is that all too frequently they don't. As with any ineffective service, the first sign is rocketing volumes of failure demand as customers who have been forced to "go digital" call the service lines because they can't get what they want from the website. This realisation – the numbers are startling – tends to prise open leaders' minds to the problem.

Agile: by what method?

Let's explore what actually happens (Deming would ask: "By what method"?) in a "digital transformation" as orchestrated by Big Consultancy.

The first step is to "incubate", which is defined as "re-imagining the customer experience". The second step is "design and pilot", or "proving the value to customers and optimising the solution on a small scale". Finally, the new digital design is "scaled", or as we would say, industrialised.

In the incubation phase, emphasis is placed on "zero-based design", in other words starting from scratch, with nothing ruled in or out. Methods used are "blue-sky thinking" and "imagination of the future", sometimes described as "imagineering" or "ideation";

---

* McKinsey Shortlist, October 5, 2018.

in short, dreaming things up. Teams do this by firstly developing "personas".

Personas are *"a kind of mental model of an imaginary person with a name, history and story who has a way of doing things. A persona"*, it is said, *"should have enough psychological detail to allow you to conveniently step over to the persona's view and see your products and services from his/her perspective. Personas are fictional, generalised representations of your ideal customer."*

New players in this process are people who describe their core competencies as "Service Design" and "Agile Delivery". Service Design is described as *"Design end-to-end services according to the needs of customers, so that the service is user-friendly, competitive and relevant to customers, while being sustainable for the service provider"*. In Agile Delivery, *"Requirements and solutions evolve through collaboration between self-organising, cross-functional teams. It promotes adaptive planning, evolutionary development, early delivery, continuous improvement and encourages rapid and flexible response to change."*

How does it feel so far? Do you think it makes sense to dream up a customer and speculate about how he or she might want to interact digitally with your organisation? How do personas help us understand what matters to customers? And is it any advantage that the people who are to turn the dreams into reality are adaptive, flexible and continuously improving?

To continue:

For each persona, the team develops, or dreams up, statements about the person's life goals, digital behaviour, financial confidence, pain points, financial portfolio, engagement with products and needs. This supposedly enables the team to understand its customers. You may be wondering how. We certainly did.

Customers are sometimes invited to sessions in which to "test" provisional designs in environments completely different from the real world. Often they are paid to attend, with the added bonus of a free lunch and drinks. The "test" consists of showing customers potential screen designs and asking them how they would feel if they had access to services that looked like the screen-shots. Not surprisingly, customers often say they like them. Seriously, this is a test?

This stage in digital transformation is what we might call the ideas stage. Whole armies of people submit ideas: service designers, software developers, Agile coaches, front-line agents, managers. Some of the ideas may work, some may not. All are collated in what is called a "backlog" – which in an Agile context simply refers to a repository of ideas (for new services, better ways of delivering existing services and, peculiarly, how to manage this "backlog" of ideas) from which tasks will be chosen to be actioned. Tasks focus on things like how to automate processing steps, send messages to customers, enable customers to upload documents, improve call-routing, change the workflow, offer online help, create new rules for transaction processing and so on – all features that can be delivered by digital technology. The culture is digital by default ("if it's digital, do it"), and the focus is on "channel shifting", automation, "going digital".

Meanwhile, the services that will be on the receiving end of these initiatives are replete with system conditions that currently *inhibit* agility. No attention is given to this. Agilists behave as if they were working in a greenfield site.

When it comes to building the new system, or part of it, the software engineers (coders) work in "sprints" – short bursts of activity – which, because sprints are time bound, means that much of the coding remains unfinished. Some of it will be added to the backlog, to be returned to (or not) at a later date.

New roles

To operate in this new culture Agilists invented a fresh methodology – "Scrum" – with new roles and rituals:

- **Product Owner**: has the executive role, deciding what a team will do. He/she is responsible for the "vision" of what's to be accomplished, taking into account risks and rewards, what's possible and what he/she is passionate about.

- **Team**: the group that will do the work; they jointly need to have the skills required to operationalise the product owner's vision.

- **Scrum Master**: the team's coach and leader, guiding the team through the scrum framework (rules and rituals) and helping the team deal with obstacles to progress.

- **Product Backlog**: a list of what needs to be done to make the vision a reality. Ideas directly concerned with developing new IT for customers are expressed as "customer stories" rather than IT development steps. The product owner is responsible for prioritising work and consulting with the team and stakeholders. The product backlog must be continually reviewed and quantified: how much effort will each task take, is there a clear "Definition of 'Done'"? Will it create value for the customer?

- **Sprint Planning**: the name given to the first of the scrum meetings, where the team, product owner and scrum master plan sprints.

- **Scrum Board**: pin- or white-board used to make work progress visible to all. It has three columns: Do, Doing, Done.

- **Daily Stand-up**: daily review of what was done the day before, what is going to be done today and any obstacles to progress.

- **Sprint Review**: meeting for the team to lay out what it has accomplished in the sprint.

- **Sprint Retrospective**: review of what went right, what could have gone better, and what will be done better in the next sprint episode.

The critical player here is the product owner, who is responsible for "optimising value" by "providing vision" and ranking the items in the product backlog accordingly. Product owners decide priorities by employing "customer research" techniques (as advocated by the Big Consultancies), including customer workshops and interviews (sometimes even interviews with non-customers). "Educated best guesses" (again with consultancy blessing) are used to create hypotheses as a basis for bare-minimum prototypes ("minimum viable product") to fire at customers and measure effectiveness. The product owner adjusts the course by nurturing some projects and killing off others according to his/her judgement of what works and what doesn't. That's how the product owner survives in his/her control system: keep to the strategic objective; be seen to be doing it the right way. Following "best practice" (the rituals) is an insurance policy. But the evidence of failure is testament to the disconnect between decision-making and what is actually happening to customers. Priorities are based on "stories" argued to represent a "vision" – which drive decisions about what is to be done.

"Epics" and customer stories

Organisational leaders are encouraged to tell big-picture stories about what is to happen, stories that are *"true, authentic, without detail and with happy endings"*. These are called "Epics". While leaders who have employed the Vanguard Method can describe with eloquence the differences between before and after a redesign, with practical examples, without any such grounding leaders of Agile initiatives dream up epics like this:

> *We look to a future where customers want and love digital means of accessing services... Our strategic intent is to delight our customers so that this channel (digital) becomes the customers' channel of choice.*

Faced with the need to comply with the strategy, Agile players let the end dictate the means. So we see epics like those above broken down into customer stories, such as *"checking my bank account online"* or *"finding out where my mortgage has got to"*. Digital designs are dreamed up for these "new" services, but because there was no knowledge of what customers actually do want, how well the current services provide it and what would create value for them, the initiatives routinely both fail to create value for customers and generate substantial unseen failure demand elsewhere in the system.

All of this occurs in the context of management's aim to drive customers into the new digital channels. They are urged on in this by Big Consultancies which frequently offer project-management controls for "increasing digital activation", complete with targets for moving transactions to the new channels. Unfortunately, numbers of transfers and transactions say nothing about how many customers like the channels, use them successfully, or believe that they create value.

The Agile initiatives fall into two broad categories: digitising steps in a service (e.g. replacing surveyors with databases) and designing new services (as with mortgage trackers). In both cases, the business case rests on the assumption that the digital element will reduce the volume of activity performed by service agents and thus deliver cost-reduction targets. We have seen instances where headcount was reduced before managers realised that activity had actually increased. Oops!

When digital channels fail to give customers what they need, it is hardly surprising that levels of failure demand hitting the service centres goes through the roof. What we've found in these cases is that the part of the organisation driving customers down digital channels to meet its "activation" targets has no knowledge of the rise in failure demand in service centres, because the latter belong to an entirely different part of the organisation. It is on someone else's budget and therefore invisible. Opening top leaders' eyes to the larger dysfunctional picture is thus the first imperative.

The choices about what to digitise tend rather naturally to be governed by what the experts think IT is good at. For example, customers often want bank statements. This looks like a simple demand, easily satisfied – request a statement and, *bing!*, here it is in the email folder. Yet requests for bank statements turn out to be much less straightforward than Agilists imagine and are often the cause of copious failure demand. Customers may need a series of statements and/or require them to be stamped for authenticity. Sometimes they need a statement for a purpose that none of the ideas merchants had imagined. So a customer might get a statement by email (tick in the box for "digital activation"), but then have to queue in a branch or call the service centre to get what they actually wanted (failure demand).

To take another example: access to many banking services requires a prior proof of income. In one digital project, Agilists designed an "income verification" process that was triggered automatically for any product requiring evidence of earnings. Understandably, this did not go down well with customers who had accounts at the bank. "What do you mean, proof of income? You see what I get every month. You know more about my earnings than I do!"

These days many organisations have adopted "chat-bots" – robots with human-sounding voices, programmed to respond to key words and phrases – often to replace IVRs (press one for this, two for that) in routing calls. The business case is generally based on assumptions that the bot will improve routing and/or increase uptake of digital services as the bot routes customers to them, and thus cut costs by reducing the need for real people.

The extraordinary thing is that in many cases the performance of the bots is "benchmarked" by the IT supplier – which is thus allowed to mark its own homework. The benchmark is calculated by measuring the proportion of bot-routed calls that are received by, for example, agents and not passed on, the assumption being that in that case the bot's routing was correct. But we know nothing from this about whether the customer's issue was actually resolved. As the Agilists have targets for digital activation, it should be no surprise that they use their ingenuity to meet them. One ploy is to incentivise agents to not pass calls on. There are a number of ways to do this. Close the call so the customer has to call in again; do anything to persuade the customer to ring off voluntarily before they realise their problem hasn't been resolved; give the customer the correct "description" of their problem and tell them to ring back and talk to the bot. The result, of course, is a rise in demand. But everyone makes their incentives. Similarly, when bots route customers to a digital service, the fact of going there is counted as digital activation; but again there is no knowledge of whether the customers' problem is solved or whether, if not, it created more failure demand.

As an aside, when helping organisations get out of such messes, which requires studying what actually happens, we find that the bot-chats are recorded, but only for the purpose of "improving routing" – getting the bot to do a better job. Compare this with the fact that the same businesses routinely record service agents, ostensibly for "quality purposes" – a wrong-headed idea to which we return in chapter 12 – yet bots are not subjected to the same scrutiny. The discrepancy speaks volumes about where management's true attention lies: cost not value and incentives not customers.

What did "Agile" do?

In cases like this, what did Agile actually do? People dreamed up ideas. Their focus was on what IT can do, treating features as benefits. Their efforts were incentivised by a regime whose focus was on "going digital". The consequence was change without knowledge. Rather than make interventions on the basis of fact, they were made under a regime that tolerated, even encouraged, failure. To argue that failure can lead to knowledge most often fails to take account of the assumptions on which the original hypotheses were built. If you're doing the wrong thing without knowing it, you won't be able to get to the right thing by studying why the wrong thing went wrong.

Agile doesn't start with questioning why performance is the way that it is. Being predicated on a philosophy of "make" (as opposed to say "improve"), the reality of the existing service is simply ignored. There is no interest in understanding how well or badly it works for customers. Instead, new digital services are ideated, designed and implemented. It should be stressed that this is not in the spirit of the original Agile manifesto. It is the consequence of a mixture of naive acceptance of the promises and fear, served by the commercial machine that, as always happens with management fads, grew up to service a new market of rituals and roles.

Agile is based on a project mentality, with work broken down into "deliverables" against date-based targets or goals, and group/team/personal objectives reported to arbitrary deadlines. Digital initiatives are set up as programmes of work – again, contrary to the principles in the Agile manifesto. Programmes and projects are common features in IT companies because their activity is primarily non-repetitive at a level of output, e.g. a licence module this week and a chat feature next. The project mentality is also favoured by Big Consultancies, since projects are the basis on which they get paid.

The digital stampede is a re-run of what happened when service centres were first established in the 1980s. Starting – as command-and-control thinkers invariably do – from a focus on lowering transaction costs with no understanding of demand from the customer's point of view simply leads to failure demand. The cost per transaction may fall, but at the price of soaring overall costs and tumbling customer satisfaction. This is the consequence of Big Consultancies selling their customers on the idea of economies of scale as a means of bringing down activity costs. But this is not a measure of effectiveness. As with many other fads, Agile has been captured by the IT and consultancy industries, by which it has been diverted from its original principles and refashioned it into a proposition that is reassuringly familiar to them and their command-and-control clients. The returns for their customers bear no relation to their investment.

Undoing the damage

The examples we have given in this chapter are taken from organisations we have helped to resist the digital mania and the groundless belief that going digital is "a do or die challenge". We'll describe how to develop effective digital services in chapter 11, but working with organisations where the problems we describe have already occurred, the first step has to be fixing the problems – you need to pay attention to what is going wrong immediately.

A look at the type and frequency of failure demand in the service centre will give a quick indication of the digital services that are falling down. The next step is to parse the current service (digital or not) end-to-end to establish whether the online offering can be improved, increasing the number of effective transactions. Where it becomes apparent that customer demands are unlikely to be met by online means, the redesign has to provide a way for customers to exit the digital channel quickly and get to a person who can help.

Digital services work well when demand is simple, predictable and repeatable; they work less well with high-variety demand. Using computers for things people are good at and people for the simple and repetitive things computers do well is to ask for, and get, the worst of both worlds. Agilists, take note.

Summary: Agile's main flaws

- An assumption that IT features are always beneficial
- No recognition of what IT should and should not be employed to do
- Dreaming-up things to create rather than grounding change in knowledge of the likely outcomes
- Roles and rituals as sufficient means – again, no recognition of the importance of knowledge as the right starting-place
- "Stories" as inappropriate representations of reality
- Governance driving delivery of IT over its effectiveness
- Proclaiming failure as a virtue

10 Is this the age of Agile?

Agile is everywhere these days. What started out as a manifesto for a better way of writing software has now spread to embrace all kinds of project management, including corporate "transformation" through digitisation. As we have seen, in principle the founding ideas are quite simple. Agile is a mind-set rather than a toolbox. It favours development by small teams, learning through fast iteration and feedback to produce successive working models. It is adaptive, responding to change, and prefers human contact to detailed processes, collaborative rather than contractual relations with customers. Who could be against being agile? Perhaps the name is part of the reason people appear to have such unswerving faith in it. Perhaps also because its predecessor as a software development methodology ("waterfall") was notoriously bad, so anything that promises to get things done faster and better seems like progress. Perhaps it is because leading names like Google, Microsoft, and Spotify are reported to be using it. But this is where the questions start. Are all organisations the same? Because Microsoft can develop new apps in short timescales, should everyone follow suit? If Spotify can design and test new ways to help users get value from their music…

Agilists are sensitive to criticism. Their attitude is, "how can one criticise something that is clearly an improvement?" Implicitly, they start from the idea, "great, the glass is 10% full", rather than, "isn't it nuts, it's 90% empty". Their judgement is based on what they have experienced. There are doubtless many examples of people having done useful things in the name of Agile, but for us a lot of it is wishful thinking.

It would be fair to acknowledge some useful Agile ideas among the many that compete for management's dollar. "Kanban", for example, places emphasis on limiting inventory and work in progress (although this is not what the term meant for manufacturers in Japan, where the idea originated). We know this is an important feature of many services that have a "project" nature, like planning applications or insurance claims. We have even applied the idea to improving productivity in software development services. But in software development, the more important question is, "Are we making the right things?" The lesson we learned – a significant one – was that it was possible to improve the productivity of software developers without having any positive impact on their customers, since the program or app did nothing to improve operations.

"Lean Startup" is another useful notion. It took a whole book* to explain one simple but important idea: when innovating, it makes sense to test whatever viable representation you can make of your offering as fast as possible. But we are not all in the business of making something new. We may be encouraged to think we are by the Big Consultancies ("forget about what you do, you're going to create a new way to do it") – but knowledge of what's going on in your current services is critical to understanding what to do next. If your objective is to knock your customers socks off with brilliant service, then a cursory study of customer demand would tell you what needs improving as well as creating urgency to act. Acting without that knowledge runs the risks we have illustrated throughout this book.

The idea of working in small teams is also good and supported by plenty of research. That it is of value in software development is no surprise to us, since we have long held the view that the ideal number for a software development team is one! But Agile, like conventional IT development, has armies of teams; a hive of activity, without knowledge of the consequences of their actions, iterating, coordinating, expediting, troubleshooting, and retrospecting. Our ideal remains one – we will come back to this.

No doubt much of the enthusiasm for Agile has been created by protagonists who evangelise its benefits. Among many, we have chosen the work of Stephen Denning, management writer and

---

* Ries, E., (2011). *Lean Startup*. Portfolio Penguin

author of *The Age of Agile,* * as the text for this discussion, his book being a good representation of the Agilist's arguments.

What's the Big Idea?

A mixture of big promises, real challenges, case-study evidence and, as ever, fear.

All large organisations are under threat, Denning warns. If they don't adopt Agile, they are doomed: hence the mantra, "digital or die". He encourages leaders

to step out of their bureaucratic, budget-management, planned and controlled system

– we wouldn't argue with that –

and simply get teams of people to ask "what is important to customers?"

How do they decide that?

then of these things what is most important?

– a good question if it's the customers' problems which inform it
– knowledge rather than guesswork –

then who are the best people to work on that?

– better to ask what we need knowledge of prior to working on it –

then ask what can be done in one month?

– but how can you know? –

---

* Denning, S., (2018). *The Age of Agile.* AMACOM

and then get on and do it without interruption.

But are we doing the right thing?

Three "laws"?

In Denning's characterisation, Agile is based on three "laws": the law of the small team, the law of the customer, and the law of the network. The small team must work in "small batches", limit work in progress, be autonomous, focus on "getting to done", hold daily "stand-ups", where they talk about what they've done, what they're going to do and raise any impediments to progress, be "radically transparent" and "retrospectively" review their work. The law of the customer translates as targeting "primary customers, experimenting, innovating in short stages, evaluating, being willing to disappoint (fail fast) and delivering value faster". The law of the network is to acknowledge that people need to work together across the organisation, employing the law of small teams. Are these really "laws"? Haven't we been here before? Are these roles and rituals necessary and sufficient for organisational agility?

A shift from seller to buyer?

For Denning, recent years have seen a massive shift in the market-place from seller to buyer. Accordingly, the firm's goal has to become one of delighting customers: i.e. a shift from inside-out perspective ("You take what we make") to an outside-in perspective ("We seek to understand your problems and will surprise you by solving them"). Agile is the means for navigating this shift.

When we watch audiences listening to this proposition, we wonder why no one shouts out, "A shift from seller to buyer? Really?" Denning cites Apple's iPhone as an example: the radically new product was hugely popular and left Nokia behind (disrupted is the new-speak). How, we wonder, is this different from Henry Ford creating a motor car – and only in black – which sold like hot cakes? Both the phone and the car were attractive to people because of what they could do for them; the new features were benefits. In Ford's case buggy manufacturers were "disrupted" and the population of horses diminished. The only example we can think of as being "seller dominated" is the communist state where production is planned centrally and people get what is made. Perhaps you could argue that management is "seller dominated" in the sense that the primary management controls are financially focused; these controls, as we have illustrated, being of no value in terms of services to customers. But this claim of a "big shift" doesn't stand up.

Reflect for a moment on the banks. While all of them have boasted for years about being "customer-focused", in truth they are nothing of the kind, their primary controls being concerned with cost, not value, the antithesis of customer-focused management. That our service organisations need agility – the ability to respond to customer demands – to survive is axiomatic. As with the banks, that's nothing new; but despite the claims and a plethora of initiatives (CRM, culture change, employee of the month, Net Promoter Score – most of which focus on people, the 5% - see chapter 12) very few deliver it. If our service organisations lack agility we are better to focus on why that is – as we did in the early chapters – rather than try to inculcate new behaviours in a system that inhibits flexibility. In the examples described in the last chapter, in one bank the net result of adopting Agile was that service went from excellent to poor, in the other from averagely poor to even worse.

According to Denning, Apple's success is down to Steve Jobs firstly getting rid of employees whose work was not adding value to customers (always sensible, and something we discussed in chapter 7) and then setting up self-organised teams. Is this sufficient evidence to justify all organisations establishing self-organising teams?

Let go of controls?

Denning goes on to argue that control is enhanced by letting go of control, another statement that ought to have audiences reeling with incredulity. We should confess that we made that mistake in the early days of developing the Vanguard Method. In a software organisation's customer services department, we knew that the measures in use (those we described in the first chapters) were dysfunctional, and we persuaded leaders to turn them off. The consequences were dire. People went to sleep. We learned the hard way never to remove dysfunctional controls without first establishing better ones – and helping people understand how to use them.

We agree that command-and-control controls are dysfunctional (that's what this book is about), and that we need a way of working that is, the way he puts it, better for those doing the work, better for those for whom the work is done, and better for the organisation – but to achieve that we need better controls, not no controls at all.

In actuality, Agile has its own dysfunctional controls. The product owner decides what to do, the team works to sprint deadlines, "digital activation" is targeted and monitored – and it gets worse. In large-scale change, there can be hundreds of small teams. When there are many teams, they have to be coordinated. This leads to the creation of yet more Agile "solutions" designed to coordinate the efforts of multiple teams across large organisations; a command-and-control thinker's dream. For example:

- SAFe stands for "Scaled Agile Framework". Note the redundant "e", but "SAF" wouldn't sell so well.

- LeSS stands for "Large-Scale Scrum" – another redundant "e".

- And DAD, which stands for "Disciplined Agile Delivery"; not quite so attractive.

SAFe, for example, promises better alignment and coordination between organisation-wide Agile teams, which could number in the hundreds or more (one large organisation has almost 20,000 people working on Agile "improvement"). SAFe merely scales up the meetings where work is planned, scheduled and reviewed. And at this, what is called the "programme level", the focus of the meetings is on "Potentially Shippable Increments" (PSI). A PSI is, typically, five sprints long. Why?

To facilitate coordination at this programme level, organisations buy or develop software to share information in what is, in effect, a project work management system. Teams can "see" their own work, and how it fits with higher levels of requirements right up to the "strategic theme". They can access all functional requirements, for all teams, notes of discussions, links to papers, information on everyone's progress, and so on. In short, they have the complete picture. A picture built from ideas. Is it the right picture? Doesn't this resemble waterfall?

If that isn't enough in terms of control, these large-scale initiatives are controlled through cost-benefit analyses, project plans, budgets and milestones, and subjected to management reviews, allocating "RAG" status to the whole and parts. Furthermore, often much of the IT development work is outsourced to low-cost providers which work to specifications and are subjected to the same controls.

In addition, we often find that features of what we might call "old-school" command-and-control software-development management have crept back into "Agile" organisations. In our language, they are system conditions governing the way software development is done. If we go back to a typical software development function, pre-Agile, it will have controls designed to serve a purpose other than creating value for customers – i.e., writing excellent software. To that end, developers are subject to targets on billed time and utilisation, and managers think, "the more we start, the more we will finish". Their obsessions are productivity and cost. But when you take time to study these systems, you find that such system conditions diminish capacity, lengthening the time tasks take, increasing the error-count and thus also costs, while disappointing customers. These controls have always been considered normal in

IT development and have naturally carried over into the new Agile environment – why would they not? When things go wrong – as they do – management's response is to add further levels of project management ("governance"), to progress-chase and prioritise, and even sometimes, "war rooms" denoting the level of crisis.

Tension between controls?

Agile teams often perceive a tension between the very different ways the teams and the company as a whole are run. Denning says this happens 80 to 90% of the time. Our experience would suggest 100%. He doesn't have much to say about the conflict other than that the old controls should go. Imagine the tension created when an operations leader works to a bonus for achieving targets for SLAs and activity times, while the product owner is incentivised for digital activation. If activation results in higher levels of demand, the operations leader will be in a pickle.

Denning tells us the new paradigm has not been easy for traditional managers to understand and implement. He says their antagonism is understandable: we would say to be expected. What actually happens is that the "old" controls remain in place, tied in as they are to the core management processes of budgeting and resource management, only downplayed – until, of course, catastrophe occurs, in which case they click back into place as the default option, the stranglehold as rigid as ever.

What help do leaders get? Denning offers little more than exhortation to get their "mindset" in order. If they don't – he is unequivocal – they can expect trouble, and Agile will flop. There has been vociferous debate, even falling out, among Agile/Scrum thought leaders in recent times, with critics – Denning among them – alarmed at abundant evidence of failure among the burgeoning training and accreditation initiatives, arguing that Agile won't be achieved with tools and processes (roles and rituals) alone. If scrum "stand-ups" and "retrospectives" are conducted under command-and-control rules, this will only lead to greater manipulation, they insist. But this is to fall into the error of assuming that command and control is about bosses being bossy. They miss the crucial point that the overriding controls in place will only serve to encourage the conventional focus on activity – so bosses will be bossy about the wrong things.

Denning describes the new mind-set as a "different way of looking, understanding, interacting, inspiring, removing impediments", and "sponsoring Agile initiatives". He gives us little more in terms of what this means in concrete terms, no useful operational definitions.

We fully agree with the critics: the explosion of an Agile training, consulting, conference and accreditation market is a dangerous diversion. Where the issue is rethinking entrenched habits, a two-day training course is emphatically not the answer. Yet the only remedies on offer here are industrial tourism – visiting places employing Agile – reading stories about others, having a go and reflecting when you do, all of which are poor or counterproductive tactics for changing thinking. The most probable result is a grafting of what they thought they saw on to their current system – the natural consequence of rational, as opposed to normative, interventions.

Denning frequently cites Peter Drucker's aphorism: "The only valid purpose of an organisation is to create a customer". With no disrespect to Drucker, we would rewrite it: the vital purpose for leaders is to gain knowledge of how their system generates and keeps customers. The starting-place is to comprehend how well or badly their current system does those things *now* – and in the case of a command-and-control system (which it will be most of the time) the leaders will be astonished how much scope there is for improvement. Moreover, provided they go and see for themselves, their mental models will change in consequence.

Spurred on by the arguments against tools and processes, and the critics' demands for a return to the founding manifesto, Scrum Alliance, a leading player in the new market, published a set of "values" for scrum. They amount to exhortations about behaviour:

focus, openness, courage, commitment and respect. We predict that it will fall at the first hurdle: focus. The values will amount to a cult-like adherence to behavioural protocols. But money will be made from yet more training and accreditation.

As we have seen, organisational agility or flexibility involves changing the system. It can't be done through the "Greater Taylorism" of digitally-enabled command and control. The evidence is abundant and incontrovertible. Paradoxically, the way people work together (behaviour and values) improves when they work in a better system, with a sound purpose and the controls we described. It all starts with knowledge, and the result is actually more in keeping with the original spirit of the Agile manifesto.

11 The Vanguard Method and developing effective digital services

Before we get on to digital services, it is important to trace our history working with information technology. Before the advent of Agile, we did a lot of work with IT developers in large organisations to change the way they worked. Often this work came about as a consequence of our having first helped to improve service operations, where IT wasn't seen as the most important thing to change and consequently was either treated as a constraint or worked around, or sometimes even turned off. Sometimes we were involved directly with IT departments either to improve the way they worked or, as in the example that follows, to solve problems with IT that fails to live up to expectations.

Studying IT development brings into clear relief the system conditions that sub-optimise performance, the chief ones being utilisation, billable time, target dates and managers' belief that the more you start the more you'll finish (which only serves to increase work in progress). You can significantly improve IT development following the archetype for effective service design with controls as we have described in previous examples. As ever, the snag is that doing things better – increasing the productivity of software developers – is not the same as doing the right things.

> *The IT development team at a large insurer was proud of its work on an intermediary web portal (a large volume of sales was brought in by brokers as intermediaries). It was delivered on time, under budget and was described as being "world class, lean and Agile". As brokers constituted an important sales channel, the chief executive would often lunch with them. He discovered a different opinion of the new portal: brokers hated it.*
>
> *As Vanguard was working there, the chief executive sent us to "sort it out". Naturally we weren't very welcome, but on*

the basis of manifest user dissatisfaction the development team was persuaded to join us in studying how the brokers worked. Together we learned how variously they operated – they had preferences for when to send notifications to customers, on whose stationery it should appear, what other information should be included according to their knowledge of customers, and whether and when it should be followed up.

So the redesign presented the now-familiar challenge: how to design a service that could absorb the variety of demand. The solution in this case was a set of rules enabling intermediaries to make choices about how the portal worked, in order to fit with the way they worked. This should, of course, have been the starting-place.

We had come to understand that doing anything to improve capacity/ productivity in software development is at best a limited ambition. Worse, players can be hoodwinked into believing that "world class", "lean" or "Agile" mean what they say on the tin. It is quite common to find examples of IT teams congratulating themselves on impeccable delivery of software that does nothing to make life easier for users, or even makes it worse.

Think back to our repairs example in chapter 8. IT vendors sell packages like the one we described for around £250,000; large organisations can spend tens or even hundreds of millions on similar systems – all designed along conventional command-and-control lines, focusing on the productivity of repair personnel, reporting things like utilisation, achievement of targets, cost of materials and so on. Large organisations typically have a centralised infrastructure of call-handlers, planners, schedulers and inspection functions, so the IT specification starts from the assumption that these functions need to be coordinated.

But as we have shown, a far more effective design is to put these functions into the front line such that leaders can exercise effective control – this being critical to profound improvement. Seeing this at the proof-of-concept design stage, leaders always ask, "But how does it scale?" What "scale" means to them is having centralised functions, when the point is that they are redundant. You don't need them. You have to remind them what they learned in the study phase: the controls exercised in these functions sub-optimise performance. Where you need control is the point at which the work is done, and those controls are focused on demand, value and achievement of purpose.

Digital "solutions"

Today, service organisations of all kinds are being sold digital "solutions". These too are driven by conventional command-and-control ideas. In housing repairs, for example, customers are given apps to report repairs, track progress and give feedback.

Leaders have heard the "digital or die" mantra repeated so many times that they are easily seduced by the offerings – they tick the box for "going digital" and they fit with the leaders' mental models. If you've followed the arguments so far, you'll know why these "solutions" don't solve anything and where to look to see why. Command-and-control digital "solutions" simply concrete over what needs to change, precluding any possibility of understanding or improving.

Designing effective digital services

The first thing to appreciate is that not every service can be digitised. As we have seen, computers work on rules; with artificial intelligence, rules that the computer makes up. Rules are not good at handling variety. Customers have idiosyncratic, personal, contextual needs. Rules work where we can predict simple, repeatable undiversified customer demands. So financial benefit in the form of lower transaction costs will be achievable in the latter case, but not in the former, where you can expect costs to rise as services are digitised.

Second, we should repeat that most "digital strategies" take no account of the obvious but neglected fact that services already exist; there is no appreciation of the extent to which they are sub-optimised and why. As we have shown, this represents a much greater opportunity for improvement than a promise conjured out of thin air. Hence our insistence that "going digital" should be moved to the back of the queue. Let's hear it once again: the rule is, IT last.

First, get knowledge

The first step is to understand the "what and why" of performance as a system. The aim is to reveal what gets in the way of the system responding to the customer's nominal value – things that inhibit agility, sub-optimise, or create costs, whichever way you want to conceptualise it. The work that ensues is knowledge-based and aligned to what matters to customers. When the system is redesigned on these terms, it will demonstrate *real* agility, in the sense of being able to respond to each and every customer's nominal value. Only then should you move on to consider what IT could do to further enhance the service. From this point, agility is built in, since measures that relate to purpose are permanently anchored. These measures keep constant track of the system's ability to achieve its purpose in customer terms. They indicate whether the actions taken for improvement – which include IT initiatives – are actually working, and will inform the focus on what to do next.

Let us now return to chapter 9's apparently simple idea of providing bank statements digitally – this time not as an example of "repairing" an ineffective digital service, but in establishing a new one. In a South African bank, studying demand revealed that requests for statements represented 10 to 15% of all demands to the bank's branches. Understanding demand isn't as simple as it might seem – the important thing is the problem the customer is trying to solve. It is a matter of context: does the customer need to prove identity, income, monies held, or something quite different? Understanding demand meant talking to customers who were asking for statements.

Knowledge of demand and context led the bank to trial services firstly on ATMs in a small number of branches (in the spirit of Agile, this could be described as *"learn*, design and test"). The ATM options reflected known aspects of demand and context, allowing customers to choose the number of statements, whether they needed them stamped and/or required confirmation they were a customer of the bank, and so on. When the new provision stabilised, the volume of failure demand fell, paving the way for an extension of the service to more branches, confident in the knowledge that it worked effectively, and to the development of an app allowing customers to access the same options remotely.

Consider how that compares with the normal approach to digitising services. Real demand – expressed in customer terms – rather than dreamed-up imaginings of the "customer journey". Studying to reveal the context and current method(s) for fulfilling customers' real needs rather than design on the basis of guesswork. All IT development focused on the value work, which is now fully understood, rather than indiscriminate software development that either remains unused or is employed in ways that make the service less effective. Finally, a much cheaper development process, since software developers are only brought into play on proven demand. Large design teams – who needs them?

Enthused by their success, the bank team started to question the way ATMs worked. When they looked at demand, they found that many customers always used ATMs to do the same thing. "What if", they thought, "we could customise ATMs so that when the customer inserted his/her card, they would be taken directly to the service they usually used, minimising the number of interactions it took to get it?" Once again, knowledge of customer demand is the lever. It tells you how individual customers want to get value from a service and teaches you which demands can be serviced most effectively by what means.

When the assumption is "IT first", investment is channelled into designing and coding; in the case of "IT last", into understanding customers. The initial batch of customers may be small, but there is intense focus on the problem(s) they want to solve and what matters to them. When a good solution is developed, it will be found to work for many more customers, broadening the research base for the second iteration. The second version works for a yet broader cohort of customers, and so on. At the beginning the process seems like a great deal of effort and time, but as it goes on it snowballs, and the goal – reducing the costs of services – is delivered by making the services more effective.

Improving the role of software developers

We have already declared our prejudice that the ideal size of a software development team is one. OK, it doesn't usually happen that way, but it is an ideal to work towards. Our second strong prejudice is that the software developers need to work *within* service operations, not separately, where they would be subject to the normal killer management controls.

> *Having made a start with the Vanguard Method to improve service operations, the attention of the leader of a Canadian telecoms service provider quickly moved on to IT, since so much of the operations work was electronic. IT developers joined in the studying and redesigning of service operations. Once the redesign was stable, and performance much improved, the question "what IT could do to further improve the system" was broached. One consequence was the elimination of waste: no code was written unless it could be clearly shown how it would benefit operations. Then a remarkable thing happened. Because they had been involved in the whole process – study, redesign, pull IT – the developers placed value on knowing how to do the front-line service work and, consequently, would happily spend time working in the front line. It kept them close to the work, which, after all, is their purpose – to improve the way the work works. Software developers like to do good work.*

Let's return for a moment to the nature of the change that had been brought about. If the developers had been told at the start that their jobs would include directly serving customers, unusual to say the least in software, how might they have reacted? Because the change was normative, it was treated as both normal and valuable.

One final example:

A South African bank's insurance division insures and maintains boilers. In some ways maintaining boilers is simpler than looking after houses, since only one type of expertise is required. Using the housing repairs template, the team took the same route to tackle the redesign of the boilers service and then went a step further. As ever, demand is the big lever. Knowledge of the boiler type, date of purchase and maintenance record can be used to predict failures. Following this line of thought, the leader began to think in terms of designing a preventative rather than a "break-fix" service – in other words, turning up before things went wrong. In practice, the effect of prevention was a sharp increase in capacity, which in turn meant that engineers could respond instantly when a fault did occur. And that became the advertising promise: "Boiler not working in the morning, we promise hot water by the evening".

Once an effective service had been designed and tested in action, it was "digitised" (note: IT last). As well as the features described above, the IT system mapped the location of the property and the position of the closest engineers. The engineer who picked up the work could then be monitored on the digital map, as was the work done and materials used on completion. Again, complete information gathered only when it was known – essential for maintaining an effective system.

The leaders called it "uberisation", because of the visibility to all parties of the customer and repairer's locations. But the real secret of its success was in the thinking, not the app.

To sum up, compare IT development in Agile (dream up, make, test) with what happens using the Vanguard Method (get knowledge, improve, pull IT as necessary).

- Agile is opinions, ideas and backlogs – tVM is knowledge first, improve second;
- Agile is mandated to implement the strategy – tVM enables strategic opportunity to emerge;
- Agile produces code first and then sees what might work, leaving much of it unused on the shelf – in tVM, code is only written that will improve the service, so none is wasted;
- Agile is high cost – tVM is low cost;
- Agile is high risk, producing poor and unpredictable results – tVM results are predictably of high value, with no risk.

This is the difference that knowledge makes.

12 Human Resources

A basic tenet of command-and-control thinking is that the difference between good and poor performance is down to people. Workers have to be instructed what to do and supervised to make sure they don't shirk or cheat and do it. As a result, managing people, optimising the use of resources – "sweating the labour" – has come to figure as one of managers' key tasks. Yet this is a massive misplacement of time and effort. The counterintuitive truth is that it is the system that governs performance. Deming taught that 95% of performance is attributable to the system, just 5% to the worker. That means that managers who concentrate on managing people are working on the 5%. Worse, when people are "commanded and controlled", the system is the greatest inhibitor to them giving their best.

Human resource departments are the relatively recent by-product of the industrialisation of service organisations along command-and-control lines. In days gone by, "personnel" departments administered pay, holidays and other benefits, but with industrialisation came the rapid expansion both in numbers and in terms of influence, of what is now labelled "HR". HR departments grew up to treat the unwelcome symptoms of command-and-control management and have steadily expanded as the symptoms have got worse and remedial efforts failed. (Here is another example of the systemic growth under command and control of bureaucracy and – sad to say, because the intent is well-meaning – of "bullshit jobs", which contribute lots of activity but in a properly designed system wouldn't need to be done at all.) Thus, having designed jobs that demoralise and disengage, we set HR people to work on measuring the extent of demoralisation and/or methods to motivate or create engagement. Ubiquitous surveys of staff satisfaction, organisational culture, employee engagement and the like can only measure symptoms. They tell us how unhappy people are, but not why. HR departments monitor absenteeism and sickness and create programmes of "absence management", but workers use their ingenuity to work out the rules – to avoid being on the wrong side of the measures

– and absenteeism remains a problem. Most HR jobs are basically damage limitation:

> *Over the last decade, UK universities have experienced a huge expansion of the "management factory" (and its pay), particularly in areas such as marketing and PR (branding, advertising) and administration (alumni management, student satisfaction, quality assessments), while academic salaries have stalled and teaching is increasingly carried out by lower-paid part-time and post-doc staff. At one prominent institution staff surveys consistently showed high levels of satisfaction with academic colleagues and motivated students, coupled with disillusion with growing administrative burdens and constant management initiatives that had nothing to do with the real work of teaching and research. The management response: to task HR with instituting a compulsory programme for academic staff on "how to cope with change".*

When measures of satisfaction or morale are poor, as is often the case, top leaders demand action to improve the numbers; a goal without a method that can only invite cheating, as departmental leaders use their ingenuity to make their unit look better. Yet the underlying reality remains the same. No amount of culture change, teamwork, values promulgation, empowerment and the like can make the experience of people working in industrialised organisations run on command-and-control methods more uplifting; such initiatives create cynicism rather than engagement. But these are the focus for HR departments as they strive to prove their professional credentials for "getting the best from people". Once again, this is doing the wrong thing righter. Far better than devising programmes to make demoralised workers happier would be redesigning work to stop demotivating them in the first place.

A new agenda for HR

Every five or 10 years, you read a major article in a management journal calling on HR to reinvent itself to make it more strategically relevant to business. But the change it needs to make – albeit a seismic one – is obvious. It needs to work on the 95% of the system that governs performance, not the 5% that doesn't. HR leaders often ask what a switch to a systems approach would mean for HR policy and practice. Our advice is not to start there, because the answer would confront them with some startling – to them – counterintuitive truths, not to mention funny looks from cynical operations folk. The starting place for HR is *after* operations have been studied and redesigned. In the face of the palpable transformation of performance and subsequent lift in morale and falls in staff absence and turnover, HR people will more easily understand how their policies and practices should be re-thought to support this new and more effective design.

The first thing HR needs to learn is how its previous policies and practice were system conditions that, despite their intent, functioned to *prevent* performance improvement. To help, they should engage in normative exercises that may have been employed to help change other managers' ways of thinking. Some examples:

The 95:5 ratio

Perhaps the best place to start, as it provides a wholly different bedrock for HR policy and practice from "people management", is to consider what it means to say that "the system governs performance".

Think back to our repairs example. Any repair operative will be dealing with the following functions in his system: call-taking, planning, despatch and materials management, each of which will be constrained by its own system conditions governing the way it works. In that circumstance, if an operative can't complete a repair on arrival, how much is he or she to blame? Equally for colleagues in the other functions – should they be "held to account" for the failure? As we illustrated, it is the system as a whole that bears responsibility. Therefore, the ability to repair at first visit will only improve when the system improves.

Here's an exercise you can do in the simplest system, the service centre. If you have one, find the activity measures currently employed to monitor and appraise agents and express them in time-series in a capability chart.* Do this for a number of workers. Your charts will look something like this one:

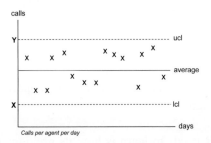

Calls per agent per day

The upper and lower control limits (ucl and lcl) are calculated from the variation between the series of data points. Following the theory of variation, this means you can now predict that the agents will take between x and y calls a day. Performance that falls anywhere between the upper and lower control limits is "normal", because this amount of variation is created by the system. It follows that, within those limits, treating a "high" (above average) performance as "better" (to be rewarded) or a "low" (below average) performance as "worse" (inviting attention) is simply wrong. This is one of the reasons why being measured and controlled in such a way is demoralising. Having a bad day is a lottery. But so is winning praise.

Agents will, of course, use their ingenuity to avoid grief and gain praise. One consequence will be that the numbers are deceptive. If incentivised (more on this later), agents will offload calls that are

---

*You can make a chart for free at: https://vanguard-method.net/capchart

not subject to the incentive, so your charts may be giving a more favourable impression than they should.

But leaving aside these issues, which regularly surface in the study phase, the next step is to identify the causes of variation. For this you will need to listen to calls, either live or recorded. For each call, ask: what makes this call go longer or shorter? Write the causes down. Your list will comprise some or all of the following: customer behaviour; compliance with processes, protocols, rules, etc; getting up to speed with e.g. marketing initiatives that the service centre isn't aware of; the IT system; activity targets and incentives; adherence to standard times; worker competence; inspection requirements, and so on. Then go through your list and ask yourself which of the causes are attributable to the system and which to the worker. You will arrive at an approximation of the 95:5 ratio: the vast bulk of the causes will be in the system.

You may be inclined to allocate any incompetence of workers to the workers themselves – as belonging to the 5%. But isn't even that the responsibility of the system? Given that leaders so rarely understand demand in customer terms and therefore cannot ensure agents are trained to meet it, is it the agents' fault that they frequently fail to meet the customer's nominal value – a concept they have probably never heard of?

This simple exercise brings HR professionals to a difficult place. They see that the many mechanisms which exist is to control the worker actually serve to increase variation, diminish value to customers and add to costs. The system is the problem, not the worker. In such circumstances, any people-management initiative is at best ineffective and at worst counterproductive – a realisation that is sometimes hard for them to accept.

> *Hayley is leader of a sales organisation, a group that is notoriously inclined to ascribe performance differences to people. The idea that 95% of sales could be down to the system was so antithetical to her beliefs that she set out to*

prove us wrong – a striking example of the human response to being told something that is completely against the grain. In fact the exercise she embarked on to prove us wrong was given to her by us.*

In studying, Hayley came to terms with the reality. She not only verified the 95:5 ratio, but she also discovered to her surprise that her "best" salespeople were actually the best at cheating to meet the incentives rather than customers' real needs.

She redesigned the sales function, removing all targets and incentives, and used her newly acquired knowledge of demand to develop her staff. Sales soared.

Incentives

Psychologists know something that managers consistently ignore: incentives systematically get you less of what you want, not more. The best review of the evidence is Alfie Kohn's *Punished by Rewards*.** When you create a contingent relationship – "do this to get that" – people focus on the "get that" even at the expense of the system, and, what's worse, the value inherent in doing the work ("do this") diminishes. You couldn't do better to create a don't-care-about-customer culture if you tried, because you make people focus on the extrinsic controls. Make the numbers, get the prize. Getting "that"– the prize – becomes the purpose.

Cheating of this kind isn't news to managers. Indeed, they themselves are adept at games-playing (particularly during the budget round), which is a normal part of life in any command-and-control organisation. That doesn't stop them from promising their superiors they will "root out the bad apples", by exerting more

---

* watch the video: https://vanguard-method.net/the-vanguard-method-and-systems-thinking/how-do-we-change-our-thinking
** Kohn, A., (1993). *Punished by Rewards*. Massachusetts: Houghton Mifflin

"control". What does become news, when managers actually look at their system to see how it works, is the extent to which the system conditions – the very controls they are relying on – are actually sub-optimising performance, creating costs and poor quality service by encouraging employees to focus their energies on hitting their targets rather than serving customers.

As Kohn shows with copious examples, incentives and sanctions (carrots and sticks) get you the opposite of what you intend. Just one of Kohn's research examples that makes you stop and think: children incentivised to read have been found to stop reading when the incentive is removed. The incentive conditions children to not-value reading.

Contingent incentives should be eliminated. On the other hand, there is nothing wrong with non-contingent rewards, like profit sharing. If the organisation does well, everyone gains.

What does motivate people?

Author Dan Pink popularised the same literature in his book *Drive**: what motivates people, he points out, is autonomy, mastery and purpose. For Deming, it was pride, joy in work, and intrinsic motivation. To repeat Herzberg's adage: "if you want people to do a good job, give them a good job to do". Our way of putting it: culture is a product of the system; *ergo*, redesign the system and culture change comes free.

Autonomy means the freedom to decide – not to be bound by rules, protocols, arbitrary measures and so on, but to be able to make judgements.

What guides judgement? Purpose – purpose defined in customer terms.

---

* Pink, D., (2009). *Drive*. New York, USA: Riverhead

Mastery means having or accessing whatever expertise is necessary to carry out the work.

All three features – autonomy, purpose and requisite expertise – are present in systems designs, whereas in command-and-control designs there are none.

One of us (Seddon) was awarded the first HBR/McKinsey prize for Reinventing Leadership in 2010. While Seddon took the prize for writing up and sending the case in response to Gary Hamel's call for innovative examples of radical management, it was actually won by the leader of the Portsmouth housing repairs service, Owen Buckwell, who created the UK's (and possibly the world's) first repairs-on-the-day-and-at-the-time-you-want service. At the awards ceremony, Seddon and Buckwell watched Daniel Pink present his thoughts. Pink's "takeaway" – US-speak for what to do about it – announced with much fanfare, amounted to letting employees have their head on the last Friday of the month.

Instead of doing whatever came into their head on Friday, Buckwell's repairs staff used their judgement every day of the week, working in a system to a clearly defined purpose and continually focused on providing the right expertise. Buckwell might have given a more illuminating presentation.

To repeat: culture change comes free. People's behaviour is governed by the system. When the system changes, so does their behaviour. The most important change in the system is in the nature of control. When that happens, people can "have their head" without risk, all day, every day. Discretion and judgement are normal and essential in an effective system.

From inspection to prevention

> *In the 1990s we were working with a large insurer. Right at the start of work in the service centre, the leader approached us to show us a revised inspection protocol that she was*

pleased to have cut down from eight pages to two. But what was on our minds was that less of the wrong thing is still the wrong thing. You can't improve with inspection – it is too late.

Many managers believe that they can improve service quality by inspecting work and providing feedback on it to agents. Unfortunately, as the Irish saying has it, "You cannot fatten a pig by measuring it". The misguided idea that you can, stems at least in part, from a disastrous misunderstanding of the concept of "quality management" in the 1980s. In the mistaken notion that quality equated to conformance to specifications, Prime Minister Margaret Thatcher was persuaded that a British standard (BS5750, a standard developed to control output which later morphed into ISO9000) could be used as a shortcut to emulate the "Japanese miracle", then at the peak of its fame. Nothing could have been further from the truth. The opportunity to understand quality theory was lost, and a parasite industry of specifiers and inspectors mushroomed instead.

The problem is that inspection focuses on adherence to the protocol, which is not the same as responding to customers' nominal values. Adherence to protocols forces agents to say or do things that are of no value to customers – it is a system condition that drives unproductive work.

To show this, inspection and feedback is a good place for HR professionals to begin studying. Take the service centre's error-rate data and express it in time series in a capability chart. Most often, you will learn that errors are low level and stable. In other words, we can predict that this system will reliably produce low levels of errors. What does that tell us about the effectiveness of the inspection and feedback process? Now listen to calls where errors occurred. How many "errors" were errors from the customer's point of view, rather than failure to adhere to internal guidance? For each error from the customer viewpoint, what were the system conditions that caused them? And that brings you back to the 95:5 system-versus-human ratio.

As discussed earlier, the systems design is based on prevention and quality – real quality, as taught by real theorists, such as Deming. In a well-designed system, responsibility replaces conformance. Leaders have the responsibility to train agents to meet predictable customer demands and provide access to expertise to meet non-predictable ones as needed. Agents have the responsibility to focus on the customers' nominal values and pull expert help as required to meet them. Designing this way eliminates wasteful bureaucracy, rids players of the emotional stress associated with inspection, and reduces errors. It also binds first-level leaders to achievement of purpose in customer terms.

Of course things will go wrong, but in a systems design they are fewer, easier to spot quickly and so simpler to repair. Leaders understand that when things do go awry, the first and most important question to ask is: "is this a predictable error or a one-off?". Treating a one-off event as a predictable one is itself a cardinal error – a sure way of stifling a system.

Appraisal

Appraisal was invented to "performance-manage" people in a command-and-control environment. In a systems design, the need for it evaporates. Particularly dangerous is the practice of ranking people's behaviours, which sets people against each other and creates a culture discouraging questioning of the status quo. Organisational correctness trumps challenge and innovation. When the causes of variation are in the system, forced distributions of performance rankings are unfair, demoralising and toxic.

People do want to know how they are doing. That conversation should be firmly grounded in the day-to-day work.

Development

Many of the conventional training programmes offered by HR are valueless and should be scrapped. "Managing poor performers" might be replaced with "How do we recognise performance variation?"; "Presentation skills" might be replaced with "How to get knowledge" and so on – but to be serious the work of people development needs to be firmly grounded in knowledge of the system. As we have seen, the nature of the knowhow needed at the point of transaction with customers emerges from an understanding of demand. Frontline staff who are used to working in a command-and-control regime will need encouragement and support to become confident enough to rely on discretion and judgement. First-level leaders' development needs are concerned with the quality of service provided on the day. All leaders need to have knowledge of the "what and why" of performance as a system, with roles designed to manage the features that enable the system to be effective (as we discussed in chapter 2).

Particular attention should be paid to new hires, especially managers. Although there is now a market for those with systems knowhow, most often new hires come with a command-and-control mind-set. Remember that leaders only come to accept counterintuitive truths through normative experiences. Frequently newcomers who have only been exposed to rational (talking) explanation get the words but not the meaning. They need to experience an "un-learn" step before they can move forward.

HR's seismic shift

To sum up: this is nothing less than a seismic shift for HR. It is no longer a function in search of a role, condemned forever to carry out fake tasks that at best smooth some of the rough edges off the excesses of command-and-control performance management. Because these fake tasks are no longer necessary it will employ fewer people, but those who remain will be fully integrated with the business, as they have long desired. The work becomes doable and, eventually, second nature when service operations have been redesigned and HR practitioners are re-focused on their role as a support and enablement function.

Epilogue

Improving UK productivity

UK productivity has been described as a vexing conundrum, and compared to G7 nations the UK deficit is the widest it has been since records began. We don't seem to know how to fix it – it is officially "a puzzle".

It isn't as though we haven't been trying. Chancellor Philip Hammond is investing £23bn with the express aim of boosting productivity, this sum to be spent on housing, roads, high-speed broadband and scientific innovation. So far so conventional – but will these investments have the desired effect, and if so, how quickly? While we may postulate links between the various means – roads and communications may make it easier to get things done, better science may in time give rise to new services and markets – they are not direct, so how confident can we be that the investment will actually drive productivity?

A sobering account is offered by Lord Macpherson, a former Treasury Permanent Secretary:

> *"All of the 34 Budgets I worked on as an official had productivity and growth as a central theme. Yet for all the interventions designed to make Britain more productive, the underlying growth rate has remained stubbornly unchanged..."* *

The Chancellor is also putting £13m into a "Productivity Leadership Group" headed by Sir Charlie Mayfield, chairman of the John Lewis Partnership. The group is described as a partnership between government, professional outfits, banks and technology firms. Not, in truth, a promising start, since none is exactly a lodestar for

---

* https://www.ft.com/content/63e057c8-fd10-11e6-8d8e-a5e3738f9ae4

productivity improvement, and at least three of the five parties have done much to harm it (no prizes for guessing which).

The leadership group reaches out to UK management with "Be the Business", a website offering benchmarking, training and coaching. Will this provide the answers?

We doubt it. Benchmarking is a high road to mediocrity – if all end up being the "best", they will also end up being the same. The argument that you can learn from comparing yourself to others is fraught with flaws. Are we really comparing apples with apples? Will the ideas of others work for everyone else? Will you perceive the things you need to see? Taiichi Ohno, the man who developed the much-lauded Toyota Production System in Japan many years ago, counselled against benchmarking for the simple reason that everything you need to know about how to improve is in your own system if you know how to look – and if you don't, it's not much use going to visit someone else's. He also joked that if he benchmarked, he'd feel inclined to stop.

We have seen that when command-and-control thinkers visit organisations that have redesigned their system, they often leave with the impression that while what they saw was pretty good ("such happy people!"), it would be even better if supplemented with command-and-control features such as targets to motivate people and, to use an example familiar to the reader, a schedule of rates in repairs systems to control costs. This is because of the phenomenon we have discussed throughout the book: what people see gets mapped on to their current mind-set, which is the very thing that needs to change. They would have been better off visiting – and joining in – when these organisations were studying their system and thereby uncovering the extent of the harm done by such practices.

Ohno also rejected the idea of "best" practice – as "best" is a static notion: a full stop. He preferred the term "better", since it is dynamic, still leaving room for improvement. The question, as Deming put it is: by what method?

The Be the Business benchmarking exercise is an online self-assessment tool through which organisations can assess leadership, employee engagement, future planning and digitisation. Oh dear. As we discussed, for many organisations the rush to digital services is resulting in anything but productivity improvement, but given its promise of lower transaction costs you can understand why command-and-control managers think it might. Employee engagement is a command-and-control preoccupation; rather, we should seek to understand why many, perhaps most, employees are conspicuously *un*engaged. Future planning is, inevitably, an inexact science if it is a science at all.

What of leadership? Be the Business offers leadership training. We agree that leadership is often at fault, mostly by leading in the wrong direction (doing the wrong things). Unfortunately, this programme, to be delivered by universities, is described as the "Be the Business Productivity through People Programme". This means that by definition it is focused on the 5% of what matters in organisational performance, rather than the 95%, which is the system. We are therefore not optimistic about the Be the Business initiative delivering anything much in the way of productivity or indeed any other improvement.

Andy Haldane, the Bank of England's clever chief economist, is another who argues that the productivity malaise is down to leadership. In his highly critical analysis, the culprits are "bad managers", whom he likens to car drivers: "Just as most people believe they are better than average drivers, so most firms believe they are highly productive." The argument resonates with us, other than labelling managers as "bad" – we would argue they are simply not aware of the dysfunction command-and-control management creates and the enormous opportunity for improvement in re-thinking management that is currently going begging.

There are other ideas for solving the productivity conundrum, for example (for listed companies) getting rid of short-term (e.g. quarterly) reporting. But that only amounts to doing less of the wrong thing. Instead we need a re-think of financial management to ensure it is grounded in knowledge of how organisations generate and use money.

We agree with other observers that companies are burdened with excessive management bureaucracy, exercising dysfunctional controls. Gary Hamel has estimated that surplus bureaucrats cost the US economy $3tn, the UK equivalent working out at £400bn. The effects of removing central bureaucracy at scale are compelling. Many years ago the chief executive of Handelsbanken simply got rid of all head office functions as he decided – rightly – that better control could be achieved at branch level, where customers are served. He also kicked out budgets and individual bonuses. Handelsbanken has outperformed European banks in terms of return on equity for 45 years.* For the same reason, Warren Buffett and Charlie Munger run the $700bn Berkshire Hathaway empire with a staff of 25 from a small office suite in a nondescript block in Omaha.

Productivity is a management problem

Most people assume that the main burden of management bureaucracy is direct overhead. But in our experience this is dwarfed by the consequential costs generated by dysfunctional controls. So while pruning egregious management bureaucracy will certainly help, the more important imperative – and the greater prize – is to treat productivity as a management problem, and more specifically one of management thinking. As we set out at the outset, national productivity is an aggregate measure of the effectiveness of our organisations at harnessing the resources at their disposal. It is axiomatic therefore that it can only be improved

* www.managementtoday.co.uk/handelsbanken-beacon-better-banking/reputation-matters/article/1437348

by better organisational performance. Private-sector organisations create wealth. Public-sector organisations consume resources. If the former create greater wealth and the latter consume fewer resources – in both cases through delivering better services – productivity and capacity will improve in a double whammy. Happier, more engaged customers and workers provide a third that is harder to measure.

The only way to do this to change the way we think about control.

Shared services: the myth of scale

The nature of the "management problem" is well illustrated by the recent fashion for sharing services, a story that conveniently brings together the main themes of this book.

Central to the command-and-control philosophy is the notion of economies of scale. Scale is thought to result in lower transaction costs, and this forms the basis for the current model of industrialised services based on service centres and back offices, built around controls on activity and cost. Since scale is everything for those who believe in it, shared services – essentially driving more volume through the same platforms – are the obvious next step.

As you will have read in our early chapters, the fatal flaw in this logic is that the transaction cost and activity measures, so rigorously tracked in the industrialised model, bear no relation to the reality of the service as experienced by the customer – in fact they actively conceal it.

This has not stopped governments around the world mandating public-sector organisations to share their admin and other services in the continuing belief that it will cut costs and transform productivity. They are actively encouraged in this by the private sector in the shape of Big Consultancy and, in particular, the IT consultancies, which have everything to gain since IT is as essential for service industrialisation as physical energy was to manufacturing.

So how have the flagship ventures in service outsourcing and sharing played out? The evidence shows a litany of failure, among the worst being government agencies (DEFRA, DfT, DWP, MoJ, UK Research Councils, Account NI…), local authorities (Northamptonshire, Birmingham, Bedford, Somerset, Liverpool, Sandwell, to name just a few), police call-handling centres and many others. Outside the UK, it is possible to uncover similarly shocking failures in public services in for example Sweden, Australia, New Zealand, and Canada. In all cases financial targets for costs and savings have been missed by a mile, while promised service improvements have obstinately failed to materialise. Some of the projects have been abandoned; in many others buyers have incurred huge extra costs to extricate themselves from costly failing contracts. In total, multiple billions of public funds have been wasted. Here is one reason why overall productivity figures are so poor.

Private-sector failures, of course, don't make the news. But there too we find similar outcomes: failure to achieve planned cost reductions alongside worse services which frequently leads to reinstatement of local provision or, in some cases, a return to the status quo. As illustrated in our first case study, we have helped many private-sector organisations to repatriate work from outsourced providers. But it's not a problem of location; it's a problem of design.

Blind to the evidence, politicians and senior civil servants remain committed to the view that sharing services will eventually pay off in economies of scale resulting in improvements to productivity. The narrative trumps evidence. Adherence to the (ideology-based) narrative parallels the manner in which command-and-control thinkers refuse to countenance counterintuitive truths. Unlike the private sector, the public sector has no rudder of profit to steer by. While in the private sector heads may roll – regardless of whether the reasons for failure were understood – public-sector leaders shrug off escalating IT costs, re-cast ("re-set) forecasts in the hope that promised savings will feed through eventually and talk of the bar being set too high, all framed by the belief that success will follow if we get the execution right. That it is the wrong thing to do is simply unthinkable.

A perfect rendition of "the narrative" was recently provided by the UK's Public Accounts Committee, which was no doubt supplied with the text by advisers, many of whom are implants from Big Consultancies and IT companies:

> *"The principles of reducing costs through using shared services are straightforward and widely understood, combining two key elements: one element is to standardise processes and services so that they can be provided in a consistent and repeatable way, in high volumes, by a single provider on a common operating platform; the other element is to outsource operations to an organisation that can specialise in providing a service and, through economies of scale, can offer the service at a lower cost."* *

If you have read the preceding chapters, you will have little difficulty in picking out the flaws in these propositions:

- *Reducing costs.* A focus on reducing transaction cost is more likely to increase overall cost.

- *On a common operating platform.* This is consultant-speak for an IT system. Recall that 90% of large-scale IT systems fail in whole or in part.

- *Standardise processes and services.* Standardised processes cannot absorb the variety of customer demand, so this step simply multiplies failure demand.

- Providing a service *in a consistent and repeatable way* should not be the purpose of a service. This is an internal focus, designed to reduce transaction costs, not to meet customer demand.

---

* https://publications.parliament.uk/pa/cm201617/cmselect cmpubacc/297/29706.htm

- *Outsource operations to an organisation that can specialise in providing a service and, through economies of scale, can offer the service at a lower cost.* Two types of economy are advanced in arguments for scale. The first is better use of a common resource – relatively speaking, fewer managers, IT systems, buildings and so forth. This is a real saving, but, in terms of economic value, a one-off and negligible in amount. In practice, it is also often hard to achieve. Lower transaction costs are always the bigger prize promised in business plans for shared services, but, as we have shown, they are based on flawed assumptions. In reality, demand always rises: great for the provider whose contract is most likely based on activity volumes and work specifications; not so great for you, when it dawns that you are in effect paying the outsourcing organisation to create and handle failure demand.

But these ("rational") challenges to the narrative cut no ice – which exposes the bigger problem, how to change the way we think about management. Only first-hand study will open leaders' minds to the flaws in the logic; an easier task in the private sector than the public, as the latter has a veritable array of players – politicians, advisers, think tanks, interest groups – sitting over public-sector leaders, completely disconnected from public services but wholly committed to the narrative. However, that may at last be changing. A recent report in *The Guardian* noted that since 2016 a growing number of local government contracts have been brought back into council control, and that many local authorities were considering insourcing services as a means of both improving quality and reducing cost. Some people believe that at local level, at least, the 40-year experiment in outsourcing may have run its course. *

---

* The Guardian, 29 May 2019, 'Why bringing services back in house is good for councils', Anna Bawden

It's the design, stupid

While this is welcome, Bower and Drucker were right: the lastingly damaging effects of command and control on our organisations can't be overestimated. The unabated fashion for sharing services brings them into sharp focus. While denial and rationalisation might be "rational" responses to uncomfortable truths, we would hope that as a leader you would at least be curious to confront and explore the evidence in your own system; that is, to risk taking a normative journey. Think of it this way: if you manage a shared service or, for that matter, any service designed along command-and-control lines, you stand on the brink of a huge opportunity. All it takes to start is to study the nature of demand in your own system – and that means doing it yourself, no delegating! When you obtain a sense of the volume of failure demand, when you see how it is for customers who need your services, when you see the effects of controls for which you as leader are responsible, a light will go on: why do we do it like this? How has it taken so long to see it? What can we do, now, to change it for the better for both our customers and ourselves?

So we come back to where we started: command-and-control service organisations are not designed to give customers what they need. We can change that.

If you drive on with understanding demand from the customers' point of view and designing a system to meet their needs, you will join many others in realising a profound improvement in revenue, service, costs and employee morale. And if you place IT at the back of the queue, rather than the front, you will find yourself rewarded with a low-cost, effective IT system which is under your control, not the other way round.

The examples in this book are a tiny sample of the profound results achieved in every type of service organisation, public or private, by taking these simple steps. Considering that more than a million people work in service centres, that even more are employed in "break-fix" organisations, and that the bulk of our economy is the service sector, the scope for significant productivity improvement needs little underlining.

And the means are straightforward. For any service, the purpose is simple, to give customers what they need. The starting-point is the realisation that meeting financial aspirations depends solely on meeting customers' nominal demands – and it doesn't work the other way around. If the results seem remarkable, it is because when we turn our theories of control on their heads, almost literally we move into a different world.

Beginning with Margaret Thatcher, UK public services have been and continue to be commanded-and-controlled by central government. Dressed up as "New Public Management", this has delivered results that are uniformly awful: high-cost, low-quality, industrialised public services that abjectly fail to meet public demand. Until the financial crash in 2008, rising investment disguised the fact that there was no underlying service improvement – how could there be when the methods were unchanged? The crash crystallised a mounting crisis. On the one hand, the environment of austerity and cutbacks bears down on service providers, while on the other the conviction of politicians and commentators of all stripes is that demand is going unstoppably up.

Which it is. But what most people fail to recognise is that the vast bulk of the increase is in failure demand – duplicated effort and expense generated by the crude and inflexible industrial model that their command-and-control methods have imposed. Ministers are at the helm, purveyors-in-chief of the pernicious central narrative, adherence to which ensures that we get the worst of both worlds: public services that consume way more resource than they should, even as they are stretched to breaking point.

Let's dispel here once and for all the myth that the private sector does it better. On the contrary: it is striking that the first, and possibly still only, repairs organisation capable routinely of delivering service on the day and precise time specified by the customer was created in the public sector. We can go further: it is the public sector that with little fanfare is leading the way here, dragging services out of the factory-based, mass-production model of the past (no wonder service centres rank as today's "sweatshops") to create the first genuinely citizen-centred services worthy of the 21st century. The people-centred services pioneered by a few brave councils, and for that matter all public services that have used the same thinking to redesign their system, are proof that it is possible not only to provide the outcomes and value for money that the authorities are desperate for, but also to refute the prevailing crisis narrative and dispel the gloom that makes using and, too often, working in public services such a dispiriting experience.

But we should not wait for policy-makers to wake up; besides, even if they did, the necessary change of heart is not something that can be mandated.* It is in the nature of this change that it has to be sought, not imposed. That's how it has grown. It is up to managers and leaders starting out with their natural human curiosity and following it up with action. It may start with local teams delivering local services to individual citizens – but, counterintuitively again, as you have seen throughout this book, productivity 2.0 isn't about scale, huge IT investment, or automation; it's about human beings working together to solve the problems of other human beings.

Humankind invented management; those who have crossed the Rubicon are reinventing it, with consequences for both our economy and our society that would be momentous.

---

* Seddon, J., (2014). *The Whitehall Effect* (chapter 14). Axminster: Triarachy Press

Index

Other books from the Vanguard stable

Davis, R., (2016). Responsibility and Public Services. Axminster: Triarchy Press

Seddon, J., (2014). The Whitehall Effect: How Whitehall became the enemy of great public services and what we can do about it. Axminster: Triarchy Press

Pell, C., (2013). The Vanguard Method in the Public Sector: Case Studies. Delivering Public Services that Work vol.2. Axminster: Triarchy Press.

Middleton, P., (2010). Systems Thinking in the Public Sector. Delivering Public Services that Work vol.1. Axminster: Triarchy Press.

Zokaei, K., Seddon, J., & O'Donovan, B., (Eds). (2010). Systems Thinking: From Heresy to Practice. Basingstoke: Palgrave Macmillan.

Seddon, J., (2008). Systems Thinking in the Public Sector. Axminster: Triarchy.

Seddon, J., (2003). Freedom from Command and Control. Buckingham: Vanguard Press.

Seddon, J., (1997). The Case Against ISO9000: How to Create Real Quality in Your Organisation. Dublin: Oak Tree Press.

Seddon, J., (1992). I Want You to Cheat. Buckingham: Vanguard Press.

Periodicals on the Vanguard Method

Three periodicals, published on the topics of Financial *Services* (2015), *People Centred Services* (2016) and *Digital services* (2017) can be found here https://vanguard-method.net/periodical/

Academic articles on the Vanguard Method

Seddon, J., & O'Donovan, B., (forthcoming in 2019). *The Vanguard Method: Beyond Command and Control.* Chapter in *The Routledge Handbook of Systems Thinking*

Pham, D.T., & Jaaron, A., (2018). *Design for Mass Customisation in Higher Education: a Systems-Thinking Approach.* Systemic Practice Action Research 31:293-310

Jaaron, A., & Backhouse, C., (2018). *Operationalisation of service innovation: a systems thinking approach.* The Service Industries Journal, 38:9-10, 561-583

Jaaron, A., & Backhouse, C., (2017). *Operationalising 'Double-Loop' Learning in Service Organisations: A Systems Approach for Creating Knowledge.* Systemic Practice and Action Research 30(4), (pp 317-337)

OECD, (2017). *Systems Approaches to Public Sector Challenges: Working with Change.* Paris: OECD Publishing

Jaaron, A., & Backhouse, C., (2016). "*A systems approach for forward and reverse logistics design: Maximising value from customer involvement*" The International Journal of Logistics Management, Vol. 27 Issue 3 (pp 947-971)

Seddon, J., & O'Donovan, B., (2015). *An exploration into the failure of Lean.* www.vanguard-method.net

Jaaron, A., & Backhouse, C., (2014). *Service organisations resilience through the application of the vanguard method of systems thinking: a case study approach.* International Journal of Production Research Vol. 52, Issue 7

Seddon, J., & O'Donovan, B., (Eds) (2014). Special issue of the journal *Systemic Practice and Action Research* (SPAR), including five articles about the Vanguard Method:

- O'Donovan, B., Editorial: *The Vanguard Method in a Systems Thinking Context*

- Dunnion, J. & O'Donovan, B., *Systems Thinking and Higher Education: The Vanguard Method*

- Gibson, J., & O'Donovan, B., *The Vanguard Method as Applied to the Design and Management of English and Welsh Children's Services Departments*

- Wilson, R., *Living the Life You Choose: The Introduction of the Vanguard Method into an Organisation Providing Support to People with Learning Disabilities*

- Watts, J., *The Perils of Command and Control*

Locality/Vanguard, (2014). Saving money by doing the right thing: Why 'local by default' must replace 'diseconomies of scale'. https://locality.org.uk/about/key-publications/saving-money-by-doing-the-right-thing/

Seddon, J., (2013). Dissolving a Dangerous Enthusiasm: Taking a Systems Approach to IT Systems, Cutter IT Journal 26.4

Seddon, J., & O'Donovan, B., (2013). The Achilles' heel of scale service design in social security administration: The case of the United Kingdom's Universal Credit. International Social Security Review 66.1, (pp 1-23)

Seddon, J., & O'Donovan, B., (2012). Process Innovation at Portsmouth Housing, in Macaulay, L.A., Miles, I., Zhao, L., Wilby, J., Tan, Y.L. & Theodoulidis, B., (Eds), Case Studies in Service Innovation (Service Science: Research and Innovations in the Service Economy), Hefley, B., & Murphy, W., (Series Eds). New York: Springer Science + Business Media

Seddon, J., O'Donovan., & Zokaei, K., (2011). Rethinking Lean Service, in McIntyre, M., Parry, G., & Angelis, J., (Eds). Service Design and Delivery New York: Springer

Seddon, J., & O'Donovan, B., (2010). Efficiencies in Public Service Delivery, in Richardson, J., (Ed.), From Recession to Renewal: the impact of the financial crisis on public services and local government Bristol: Policy Press

Seddon, J., & O'Donovan, B., (2010). Why aren't we all working for Learning Organisations? AMED e-Organisations and People 17.2

Zokaei, Z., Elias, S., O'Donovan, B., Samuel, D., Evans, B., & Goodfellow, J., (2010). Lean and Systems Thinking in the Public Sector in Wales. Lean Enterprise Research Centre report for the Wales Audit Office Cardiff University

Seddon, J., (2009). Failure Demand – from the horse's mouth. Customer Strategy 2.1 Winter 2009, (pp 33-34)

Advice UK, (2009). Interim Report: Radically Rethinking Advice Services in Nottingham London: AdviceUK

Advice UK, (2008). It's the System, Stupid! Radically Rethinking Advice London: AdviceUK

McQuade, D., (2008). Leading Lean Action to Transform Housing Services. Public Money and Management 28.1

Seddon, J., & Brand, C., (2008). Systems Thinking and Public Sector Performance. Public Money and Management 28.1

Pyke, W., (2008). Is performance personal or in the system? Management Services 52.4 Winter 2008, (pp 40-47)

Jackson, M., Johnston, N., & Seddon, J., (2008). Evaluating Systems Thinking in Housing. Journal of the Operational Research Society 59, (pp 186-197)

Seddon, J., & Caulkin, S., (2007). Systems thinking, lean production and action learning. Action Learning Research and Practice 4.1 (April 2007), special issue: Lean Thinking and Action Learning

Office of the Deputy Prime Minister, (2005). A Systematic Approach to Service Improvement Evaluating Systems Thinking in Housing. London: ODPM Publications

If you want to get started

The advantages in engaging a Vanguard expert are speed, being focussed on the right things and not making the mistakes we have made; as Ackoff always said: if you're doing the wrong thing and trying to do it right you'll not learn from your mistakes. There are many ways you can connect to our mentors, and through them our e-learning system which includes extensive examples and applications. Whether you are already on the journey beyond command and control and need somebody to keep you honest (or sane!) or need support to undertake a system redesign, we provide over 35 years of experience and guidance in the steps for study, redesign and sustaining new systems designs. Vanguard also provides an accreditation service for both in-house practitioners and consultants. This gives you access to a Vanguard expert who will help you develop, and acknowledge, your competence in applying the Vanguard Method.

We would advise against employing people who purport to be competent in the Vanguard Method. We have seen some shocking examples of consultancies misunderstanding and wrongly interpreting our work. You'd be better off trying to work it out for yourself! To return to Ackoff: if you're doing the right thing wrongly you *will* learn from mistakes.

About the authors

John Seddon is a respected and outspoken management thinker and commentator. Trained as an occupational psychologist he has become an international authority on service organisations. John has received numerous academic awards for his contribution to management science; he is currently a Visiting Professor at Buckingham University Business School and was awarded the first Management Innovation Prize for 'Reinventing Leadership' in 2010. John was described by the *Daily Telegraph* as a "reluctant management guru".

John Seddon

Ibrar Hussain

Together with his colleagues John developed the Vanguard Method; the means by which they help leaders of service organisations change from a command-and-control design to a systems design, ensuring leaders make decisions on the basis of free and informed choice.

Ibrar Hussain, Toby Rubbra and Barry Wrighton are leaders of the Vanguard organisations, currently operating in eleven countries.

Toby Rubbra

Barry Wrighton